MORE
CREATIVE INTERVENTIONS
FOR
TROUBLED CHILDREN & YOUTH

LIANA LOWENSTEIN

Champion Press
Toronto, Canada

More Creative Interventions

© 2002 Liana Lowenstein

Printed in Canada by Hignell Book Printing.

National Library of Canada Cataloguing in Publication Data

Lowenstein, Liana, 1965-
    More creative interventions for troubled children and youth/Liana Lowenstein

Includes bibliographical references.
ISBN 978-0-9685199-1-2

1.Play therapy. 2. Child psychotherapy. 3. Adolescent psychotherapy.
4. Group psychotherapy for children. 5. Group psychotherapy for teenagers.
I.Title.

RJ505.P6L683 2002   618.92'891653   C2002-903799-9

Correspondence regarding this book can be sent to:
Liana Lowenstein c/o Champion Press
Pharma Plus, 2901 Bayview Avenue, PO Box 91012, Toronto, Ontario, Canada M2K 1H0
Telephone: 416-575-7836
Email: liana@globalserve.net Web: lianalowenstein.com

ACKNOWLEDGMENTS

I am forever grateful to the many children who, during my years of clinical practice, have touched and enlightened me. They continue to be my inspiration. My heartfelt thanks to Trudy Post-Sprunk, Scott Riviere, and Janine Shelby, who so generously donated their time to review my manuscript, and who provided me with invaluable feedback on the text and the activities. In addition, I wish to thank the many talented colleagues who graciously took the time to try the activities with their clients, and who provided me with suggestions and words of encouragement. A special gratitude to Jennifer Meader, who wrote *Participaction: A Story About Bullying*. Thanks also to Karen Payton, for her careful editorial assistance, and to Dave Friesen From Hignell Printing, for his helpful input. Finally, I wish to thank my husband, Steven, and my family and friends for their ongoing support.

TABLE OF CONTENTS

ACTIVITIES AT A GLANCE

ACTIVITY	THEME	AGES	MODALITY
The I Don't Know Game	Engagement/Assessment	6+	Individual
Paper Bag Puppets	Engagement/Assessment	4-10	Individual, Group, Family
About Me Puzzle	Engagement/Assessment	7+	Individual, Group
Scavenger Hunt	Engagement/Assessment	6+	Individual, Group
Color The Circle	Engagement/Assessment	10+	Individual, Group
The Way I Want It To Be	Engagement/Assessment	7+	Individual, Group, Family
Letting The Cat Out Of The Bag	Feelings	4-8	Individual, Group, Family
Feeling Faces Coloring Book	Feelings	4-8	Individual, Group
Guess Which Cup	Feelings	6-12	Individual
Go Fish	Feelings	6-12	Individual, Group, Family
Anti-Stress Kit	Feelings	10+	Individual, Group
Theme Song	Feelings	12+	Individual, Group, Family
Brainstormers	Anger Management	9+	Individual, Group
If You're Mad And You Know It	Anger Management	4-6	Individual, Group, Family
Anger Workbook	Anger Management	9+	Individual, Group, Family
Road Rage	Anger Management	7-12	Individual, Group, Family
Rate It	Anger Management	9+	Individual, Group, Family
Don't Flip Your Lid	Anger Management	7-12	Individual, Group
Bubbles	Social Skills	4-6	Group
Kerplunk	Social Skills	7-12	Individual, Group
Getting Along With Others Game	Social Skills	7+	Individual, Group, Family
Participaction: A Story About Bullying	Social Skills	7-12	Individual, Group
MVP (Most Valuable Player)	Social Skills	7+	Group
Flip A Coin	Social Skills	9+	Group
Happy Birthday	Self-Esteem	4+	Group, Family
Turning Over A New Leaf	Self-Esteem	9+	Individual, Group
Labels	Self-Esteem	9+	Group, Family
Light Up Your Life	Self-Esteem	12+	Individual, Group, Family
Gift Bag	Self-Esteem	9+	Individual, Group, Family
Pizza Party	Self-Esteem	7+	Individual, Group, Family

PREFACE

The success of *Creative Interventions for Troubled Children & Youth* published in 1999 demonstrated clinicians' need for innovative, practical, therapeutic activities. *More Creative Interventions for Troubled Children & Youth* presents new techniques for practitioners to add to their existing therapeutic repertoire. As in the first volume, games, art, puppets, music, role-plays, and stories are used to engage children and youth in the counseling process and help them work through their treatment issues.

The activities in this book are divided into five chapters: Engagement and Assessment, Identifying and Coping with Feelings, Anger Management, Social Skills, and Self-Esteem. The book begins with engagement and assessment activities providing clinicians with practical ideas to build rapport and gain useful client information. The remaining four chapters provide treatment activities to help children master key emotional and behavioral competencies such as identifying feeling states, coping with emotional difficulties, managing anger, strengthening interpersonal skills, and enhancing self-esteem. A variety of activities are provided within each chapter, so that practitioners can choose interventions that suit their client's specific needs. Appendix A presents rituals for check-in and check-out for use at the beginning and end of counseling sessions. Appendix B includes practical techniques to help therapists better manage challenging clients.

The activities in this book are described within a framework that recommends age suitability, preferred treatment modality, and appropriate stage of treatment. Materials needed to complete the activity are outlined. (The resource section at the back of the book details where particular materials may be obtained.) Several activities include worksheets that may be reproduced for use with clients. The book includes detailed instructions for all activities and a discussion section that further clarifies both application and process.

Some of the exercises are only appropriate for use in one particular modality, such as individual or group treatment. Other activities are suitable for various modalities and can be modified. Group exercises can be adapted for use in family and multifamily group sessions. For activities that are used primarily in an individual or group context (rather than in a family therapy setting), consideration should be given to the manner in which the child's caregivers and larger community will be involved in the treatment. Effective treatment, however, often requires a systemic approach, therefore, every effort should be made to involve the child's family and community in the treatment. Making therapeutic contracts with the child, the child's family, and community agencies can address issues related to client involvement, communication, and confidentiality.

Each activity recommends a suitable client age range. However, some children with developmental delays or learning disabilities may lack the capacity to respond appropriately to a particular activity. If this is the case, the activity may need to be altered to fit the child's developmental capacities.

While detailed descriptions are provided regarding the activities in this book, the activities can be adapted to suit the distinct treatment needs of each child. Creativity and flexibility are strongly encouraged, so that children are responsive to each intervention, and therapeutic goals are achieved.

It is gratifying to know that the original *Creative Interventions for Troubled Children & Youth* was a valuable resource for so many therapists. I hope this book is equally useful, and the activities create an engaging and meaningful therapeutic experience for your clients.

Liana Lowenstein

GUIDELINES

The purpose of this book is to provide mental health practitioners with innovative activities to engage, assess and treat children, youth, and families. In using these activities however, the following guidelines should be considered:

Be Well Grounded In Theory and Practice

Mental health professionals using this book should have clinical training and a sound knowledge base in the following areas: child development, psychopathology, child management, art and play therapy, and group counseling. A list of suggested readings and professional training associations is provided at the end of this book for those who wish to broaden their knowledge.

The activities in this book can be integrated into any theoretical orientation that uses a directive child therapy approach. Thus, practitioners from a wide range of theoretical orientations will find many activities in this book to incorporate into their counseling sessions.

Build and Maintain A Positive Therapeutic Rapport

All children need relationships which provide them with a feeling of security, acceptance, and self-worth. For children who enter therapy, this is even more significant because these children typically have a damaged sense of self and many have few social supports. In order to form a therapeutic relationship, the therapist must be non-judgmental and convey a sense of empathy and respect for the child. The rapport that develops between therapist and child forms the foundation for therapeutic success.

Involve the Child's Caregivers

Whenever possible, the child's primary caregiver should be involved in the treatment. The caregiver may be a parent, stepparent, foster parent, grandparent, childcare worker, or some other adult responsible for the care of the child. Lack of follow-through with treatment, or premature termination of the child's treatment, is less likely if the caregivers are part of the process.

The caregiver can play a critical role in helping the child work through treatment issues. Moreover, caregiver involvement can help reduce the child's feelings that he is the "damaged" one. The extent to which the caregiver becomes involved in the child's treatment should be based on the abilities of the caregiver, the caregiver's motivation, and the child's needs.

Select Activities That Fit the Child's Needs

There are a variety of activities to choose from in this book. The child's interests and abilities should be considered to ensure that the selected activity appeals to her and sustains her motivation. Select activities to fit the child's treatment goals. Pacing is also important. Implement engagement and assessment activities before activities that are more emotionally intense, or that require the client to take greater emotional risk. Ending activities should consolidate the skills learned during therapy, encourage the child's independence, and celebrate the client's realization of treatment goals.

If an activity is used in a group or family context it should fit the interests, functioning levels, and treatment needs of each of the members.

It is also important to be aware of cultural issues. The therapist should become competent in multicultural counseling and utilize interventions that are culturally sensitive.

Be Process Focused

The play-based activities in this book make it is easy for both therapists and children to enjoy the sessions and forget about the process and treatment objectives. Therefore, therapists must remember that these activities are tools for intervening therapeutically with troubled children. So, by all means create a playful atmosphere, but implement the activities carefully, thoroughly, and sensitively, always keeping in mind the child's treatment objectives.

The therapist should consider how to introduce, process, and bring closure to each activity. When introducing an activity, the therapist should be enthusiastic in order to engage the client. The purpose of the activity should be outlined and the instructions clearly explained. As the child moves to a more engaged and ready state, deeper issues can be skillfully explored and processed. When the activity has been completed and sufficiently processed, the therapist provides positive feedback to the child on his completed work and brings closure to the activity. The therapist should help the client explore how to apply the skills learned in the session to situations outside the therapy setting.

In addition to considering how to introduce, process, and bring closure to an activity in a particular session, the practitioner must also be concerned with the impact of the activity on the client beyond the session. Although some activities are designed to bring issues and feelings to the surface, care must be taken to ensure that the child does not leave the session feeling overly stressed or unsupported.

Set Firm But Fair Limits

Lack of boundaries and controls during a treatment activity can overwhelm the child and lead to feelings of heightened anxiety. As such, there is a need to provide the child with limits and structure. The nature and intensity of the limits will depend on the child's existing capacity for self-control, as well as his responsiveness and ability to handle such limits.

Practitioners may feel overwhelmed when children test limits or engage in difficult behaviors. There is a special section in the appendix to provide therapists with suggested techniques to better manage challenging client behavior.

Be Aware of Transference and Countertransference

Transference occurs when a child displaces patterns of feelings and behavior originally experienced with other significant figures onto the therapist. When transference is maladaptive, inappropriate, or prevents a child from healthy growth and development, the therapist must focus on helping a child to establish new interactional patterns.

Counter-transference is the unconscious influence a therapist's past needs and conflicts have on his or her understanding, actions, or reactions within the treatment situation. Therapists need to have insight into their own personality dynamics so that their unconscious issues do not become a hindrance to the therapeutic process.

Transference/counter-transference issues are often difficult for the therapist to deal with. The therapist may find it useful to obtain guidance from a skilled supervisor, consultant, or co-worker.

Be Creative

The creative and imaginative use of structured activities, games, and exercises is a source of fun, play, and enjoyment for children. The activities in this book are designed to appeal to children so they will embrace therapy and have a positive counseling experience. Therapists are encouraged to be creative and modify the activities to meet the distinct needs of their clients.

CHAPTER ONE:
ASSESSMENT ACTIVITIES

Each new client presents unique emotional, cognitive, and behavioral issues. Many children have difficulty verbalizing their presenting issues because they are reluctant to self-disclose and they are anxious about the therapeutic process. Activities that are creative and play-based can engage otherwise resistant children and can help them express their thoughts and feelings. This chapter provides a number of activities that can be used to engage and assess clients. While these activities provide useful strategies to engage children, it is the therapist's use of self that is the most powerful engagement tool. The therapist's warmth, consistency, and unconditional acceptance of the child are the key ingredients to put children at ease and help develop a therapeutic rapport.

THE "I DON'T KNOW, I DON'T CARE, I DON'T WANT TO TALK ABOUT IT" GAME

Theme: Engagement and Assessment
Recommended Age Range: Six and Up
Treatment Modality: Individual
Stage of Treatment: Beginning, Middle

Goals
- Engage and assess the client
- Create a safe environment for the client to share ideas, feelings, and behaviors
- Establish a therapeutic rapport
- Facilitate communication

Materials
- Small bag of potato chips

Advance Preparation
Obtain permission from the child's caregiver to offer food.

Description
The therapist explains the game as follows:

We're going to play a game that's going to help us get to know each other. It's called the I Don't Know, I Don't Care, I Don't Want to Talk About It Game. I'm going to begin by asking you a question; a question that will help me get to know you better. If you answer it, you get a chip, but if you say I don't know or I don't care or if you don't answer the question, I get your chip. Then you get to ask me a question. If I answer the question, I get a chip. But if I say I don't know or I don't care or if I don't answer the question, you get my chip. The game continues until we've asked each other ten questions.

Discussion
Most therapists who work with children have encountered the I-don't-know child. These clients can be difficult to engage and a challenge to assess. This activity helps to break through the resistive barrier.

The order and pacing of questions in this game is important. The therapist should begin with neutral questions such as, "What do you like to do when you are not in school?" and "What is your favorite color?" Feelings questions can come next, such as, "What is something that makes you feel happy?" and "How do you feel about being here today?" As the child begins to feel more at ease, questions that involve greater risk taking can be asked, such as, "What's something you wish you could change about your family?" and "Why do you think you're here today"? (Since this is an engagement activity, the therapist should be in tune with the client's readiness to answer questions that may feel threatening.) End the game on a positive note with a question such as, "What's your happiest memory?"

The therapist should handle the child's questions with discretion. Some self-disclosure is required, but only information that is appropriate and helpful to the child should be shared. If the child chooses not to answer a question, the therapist can respond, "You must know yourself really well; you know what you feel comfortable talking about and what you want to keep private for now." This is an empowering message for the child.

PAPER BAG PUPPETS

Theme: Engagement and Assessment
Recommended Age Range: Four to Ten
Treatment Modality: Individual, Group, Family
Stage of Treatment: Beginning, Middle

Goals
• Engage and assess the client
• Create a safe environment for the client to share ideas, feelings, and behaviors
• Increase verbal and non-verbal communication
• Establish a therapeutic rapport

Materials
• Paper bags
• Decorative supplies i.e., markers, cloth, colored yarn, googly eyes, lace, ribbons, etc.
• Glue stick
• Child-safe scissors

Description
The therapist and child each make a paper bag puppet to represent themselves. Once the puppets have been created, the therapist and child introduce their puppets. Next, the therapist uses the puppets to interview the child asking questions such as:

What is your name?
How old are you?
Who do you live with?
What is your favorite color?
What is your favorite toy?
What is your favorite food?
Are there any foods you hate?
If you had three wishes, what would you wish for?

Discussion
Children will enjoy constructing their puppets. The informal discussion that arises during the puppet construction phase, coupled with the information gathered during the interview, will provide useful assessment material. Using puppets creates a safe distance for children and elicits information that they may not readily express directly. The puppets can be used in later sessions to help children communicate and act out scenarios relevant to their treatment issues.

ABOUT ME PUZZLE

Theme: Engagement and Assessment
Recommended Age Range: Seven and Up
Treatment Modality: Individual, Group
Stage of Treatment: Beginning, Middle

Goals
• Engage and assess the client
• Create a safe environment for the client to share ideas, feelings, and behaviors
• Establish a therapeutic rapport
• Increase awareness of personal uniqueness

Materials
• *One About Me Puzzle* for each client (included)
• Cardboard or heavy colored paper
• Glue stick
• Scissors
• Clear tape
• Magazine pictures
• One envelope for each client

Advance Preparation
Photocopy the puzzle and glue it onto a piece of cardboard or heavy colored paper. Glue a magazine picture appropriate to the child's interests onto the other side. For example, a picture from a sports magazine might appeal to a child who enjoys sports, while another child might enjoy a picture of animals. Cut the puzzle along the dotted lines and place the eight pieces in an envelope.

Description
The therapist gives the child the puzzle. The child completes the puzzle by writing a response to the first question and progressing to question number eight. (If this activity is used with younger children, the therapist can transcribe the child's answers.) Once a response has been written for all eight questions, the child can assemble the puzzle and tape it together. The child can then turn the puzzle over to uncover the picture.

Discussion
This activity offers a simple yet engaging way to get to know the child. It is a good starting point in therapy and sets the tone for creative strategies to elicit information from clients. Therapists can be innovative in their selections for the puzzle, individualizing them to meet each child's unique needs. Use pictures from magazines such as, *Sports Illustrated, Teen People, National Geographic,* or perhaps the comics from the newspaper or a page from a joke book.

ABOUT ME PUZZLE

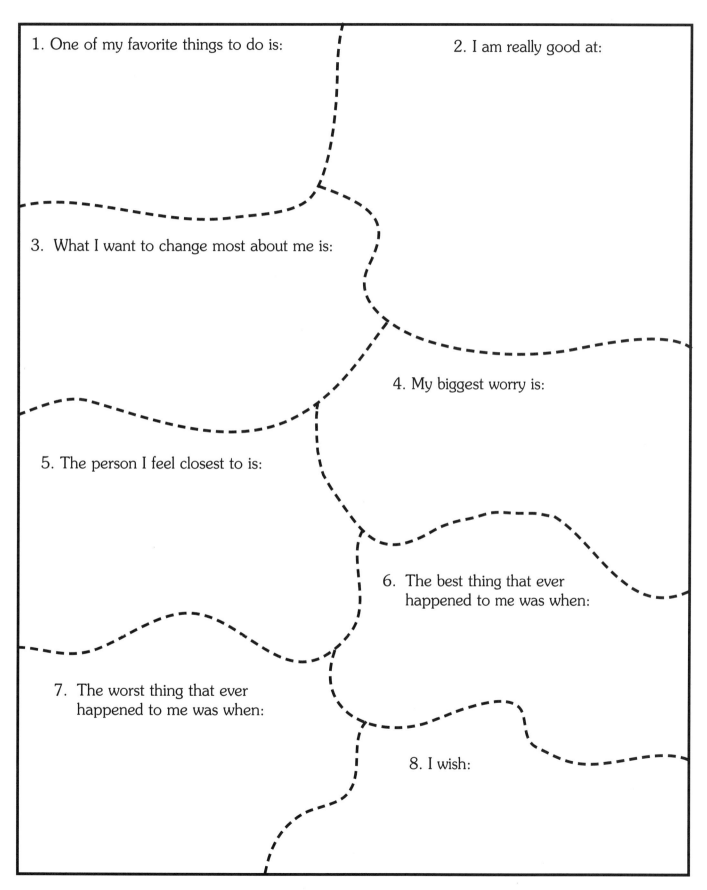

1. One of my favorite things to do is:

2. I am really good at:

3. What I want to change most about me is:

4. My biggest worry is:

5. The person I feel closest to is:

6. The best thing that ever happened to me was when:

7. The worst thing that ever happened to me was when:

8. I wish:

SCAVENGER HUNT

Theme: Engagement and Assessment
Recommended Age Range: Six and Up
Treatment Modality: Individual, Group
Stage of Treatment: Beginning

Goals
• Engage and assess the client
• Create a safe environment for the client to share ideas, feelings, and behaviors
• Facilitate communication
• Establish a therapeutic rapport

Materials
• One *Scavenger Hunt* booklet for each client (included)
• Glue stick
• Scissors
• Markers or crayons
• Assortment of magazines with pictures i.e., *Sports Illustrated, Teen People, National Geographic*, mail order catalogues, newspapers, etc.

Advance Preparation
Make copies of the *Scavenger Hunt* booklet for each client.

Description
The therapist begins by asking the child, "Have you ever been on a scavenger hunt?" and the child can share her experiences. Next, the therapist explains this special version of the scavenger hunt:

You will be given a booklet with a list of items to include. You are not allowed to write the names of the items but you can draw pictures or find pictures from the magazines.

The therapist then gives the *Scavenger Hunt* booklet to the child to complete (if used in a group then each child gets her own booklet). The child then explains the pictures she drew or pasted in the booklet, and shares her likes/dislikes, feelings, etc.

A fun way to close this activity is for the child to collect the following scavenger hunt items:
• Left shoe
• Something green
• Funny sound
• A good deed
• Something soft
• Outline of a hand
• Drawing of the therapist
• Verse from a song

• Funny face
• A joke

For a group the leader divides the children into teams and has each team race to collect the items.

Discussion

This activity facilitates communication from non-verbal or resistant children. It enables clients to reveal information about themselves, and to identify treatment goals. Information gathered through the activity will provide the therapist with direction for future treatment.

The *Scavenger Hunt* booklet can be modified to collect other information. For example, the booklet can focus on a particular treatment issue, such as the death of a parent. Items in the booklet can include:

How I felt when my parent died
A happy memory of my parent
Something that helps me now

SCAVENGER HUNT

Something I Enjoy Doing:

My Favorite Food:

How I Feel About Coming To Therapy:

A Problem I Need Help With:

What I'd Like to Change About My Family:

A Wish I Have for Myself:

COLOR THE CIRCLE

Theme: Engagement and Assessment
Recommended Age Range: Ten and Up
Treatment Modality: Individual, Group
Stage of Treatment: Beginning

Goals
• Engage and assess the client
• Facilitate communication
• Establish a therapeutic rapport
• Develop individual goals

Materials
• One *Color the Circle* worksheet for each client (included)
• Pencil or markers

Advance Preparation
Copy one *Color the Circle* worksheet for each client.

Description
The client completes the worksheet then discusses it with the therapist.

Discussion
This activity provides valuable assessment information. The therapist is able to gain a more accurate understanding of the client's thoughts and feelings when they color in the circles to represent how strong their individual feelings are about specific issues. This is a particularly useful activity with clients who have difficulty articulating their feelings because the client can communicate salient information without having to verbalize. The therapist can use the client's responses as a point of departure for further discussion.

Worksheet
COLOR THE CIRCLE

Read each statement below and fill in the circles to show how you feel. If you totally agree, color in the whole circle. If you agree a bit, color in part of the circle. If you don't agree at all, leave the circle blank.

It's hard for me to talk about my problems:

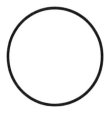

I pretend that everything is okay even when I feel upset:

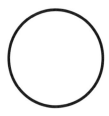

I feel loved and cared for:

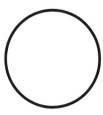

I get along well with my family:

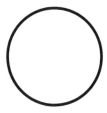

I get along well with other kids:

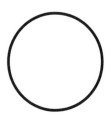

I think my family needs help:

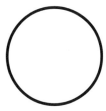

I am worried I won't do well in school:

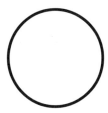

I feel I am a good person:

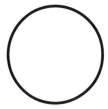

There are things that I do well:

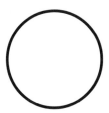

I am glad I am getting help now:

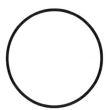

THE WAY I WANT IT TO BE

Theme: Engagement and Assessment
Recommended Age Range: Seven and Up
Treatment Modality: Individual, Group, Family
Stage of Treatment: Beginning, Middle

Goals
• Engage and assess the client
• Increase awareness of presenting problems
• Facilitate development of treatment goals

Materials
• Two large pieces of paper
• Markers

Advance Preparation
Write at the top of one of the pieces of paper: The Way My Life Is. Write at the top of the second piece of paper: The Way I Want It To Be.

Description
The client draws two pictures. The first on the sheet of paper is titled The Way My Life Is. The second on the sheet of paper is titled The Way I Want It To Be. The client then discusses the two pictures. The therapist can ask the following process questions:

How did you feel during the drawing activity?
How are you going to get from the way it is to the way you want it to be?
What do you need to do differently in order to get to the way you want it to be?
How might therapy help you get to where you want to be?
How will you feel when you get to where you want to be?

A variation for family therapy is to have the family draw two pictures. The first is titled: The Way It Is In Our Family. The second is titled: The Way We Want It To Be. The therapist processes the activity as above, but the questions are reworded to suit family therapy. Suggested questions include the following:

How did each person in the family feel during the drawing activity?
How is your family going to get from the way it is to the way you want it to be?
What does each member of the family need to do differently to help your family get to the way you want it to be?
How might therapy help your family get to where you want to be?
How will it feel to get to where you want to be?

Discussion

A client's artwork can be used in counseling sessions as tools for assessment and creative expression. Through the expressive arts medium, a client's thoughts, feelings, and experiences are translated into concrete images. This drawing exercise enables a client to examine presenting issues and define treatment goals for future intervention.

Incorporating art activities into family sessions provides a medium to engage all family members. While the content of the family drawings provides valuable diagnostic information, the therapist should also focus on the family dynamics that emerge during the exercise, for example:

What role does each person play in the family?
Did the interaction take on structure, or was it chaotic?
Did any dysfunctional patterns emerge, for example, parentification, triangulation, disengagement, scapegoating, overfunctioning?

CHAPTER TWO:
IDENTIFYING AND COPING
WITH FEELINGS

Many children lack the emotional, cognitive and verbal abilities to communicate their feelings directly. Children may also suppress their feelings, or restrict their feelings vocabulary to happy, sad, and mad. In such cases, children need permission to express themselves openly and enhance their feelings vocabulary so they have a means of identifying a range of feeling states.

When children are limited in their ability to talk about their feelings, it can help to combine discussion with engaging play-based activities. The structured play activities in this chapter include games, music, expressive arts, and psychodrama, to help children verbalize and express their feelings with lowered levels of anxiety. Activities that address stress management and healthy coping styles are also included in this chapter to assist children in dealing more effectively with overwhelming experiences.

LETTING THE CAT OUT OF THE BAG

Theme: Identifying and Coping with Feelings
Recommended Age Range: Four to Eight
Treatment Modality: Individual, Group, Family
Stage of Treatment: Middle

Goals
• Encourage greater awareness of feelings
• Facilitate the healthy expression of feelings
• Increase feelings vocabulary

Materials
• Non-transparent bag
• Stuffed toy cat

Description
The stuffed cat is placed in the bag. The therapist and child take turns being Actor and Guesser. (If this is a group activity, then the participants can take turns being the Actors while the other members act as Guessers.) The Actor chooses a feeling, such as excited, then pulls the cat from the bag with an excited facial expression and body movement. The Guesser must guess the feeling. Roles are then reversed. The activity continues until each player has had several turns and various feelings have been enacted.

It might be helpful to provide younger children with a list of feelings to choose from. The list can be reviewed before each round. Feelings that can be included are excited, disappointed, afraid, mad, yucky, confused, surprised, etc.

Discussion
This activity provides young children with the opportunity to develop a vocabulary for their feelings and to practice expressing those feelings. Children typically become more animated as the activity unfolds. The therapist can praise the children for the appropriate expression of affect by making comments such as, "Wow! You can really show your feelings!"

FEELING FACES COLORING BOOK

Theme: Identifying and Coping with Feelings
Recommended Age Range: Four to Eight
Treatment Modality: Individual, Group
Stage of Treatment: Middle

Goals
• Encourage greater awareness of feelings
• Facilitate the healthy expression of feelings
• Increase feeling vocabulary
• Assess client

Materials
• One *Feeling Faces Coloring Book* for each client (included)
• Several *Feeling Faces* sheets for each client (included)
• Crayons
• Child-safe scissors
• Glue sticks

Advance Preparation
Photocopy one *Feeling Faces Coloring Book* for each client. To make a booklet for each child, cut out the eight squares on the four coloring book pages and staple them together in order, from one to eight. Make several photocopies of the *Feeling Faces* sheet for each client.

Description
The therapist explains to the child that they are going to make a coloring book about feelings. The child begins by decorating the first page of the coloring book. The feeling faces are then reviewed and explained (younger children will understand happy, sad, mad, and scared but may need an explanation for nervous and guilty). The therapist reads each page of the coloring book to the child. The child completes each page by cutting out the feeling face(s) that corresponds with how he or she feels. Note that there is ample room on each page for children to glue more than one feeling face. The therapist may wish to highlight the fact that people often experience more than one feeling at a time. The feeling faces are glued onto each page and the child can color in the faces. The booklet can be used as a point of departure to discuss the child's feelings.

Discussion

This activity provides young children with a vocabulary to verbalize their feelings. Children will enjoy the cut and paste format of the activity and will gain a sense of mastery as they create their personalized coloring books.

The therapist may wish to adapt the coloring book to suit the treatment needs of the client. For example, if the child witnessed domestic violence, questions can be included such as, "When mommy and daddy were fighting I felt..."

Worksheet
FEELING FACES COLORING BOOK

- 1 -

_____'s
Feelings Book

- 2 -
When I play with my favorite toy I feel:

- 3 -
When I play with other children I feel:

- 4 -
When I am with my family I feel:

- 5 -
When I get in trouble I feel:

- 6 -
When I get hurt I feel:

- 7 -
When I have a bad dream I feel:

- 8 -
When it's my birthday I feel:

FEELING FACES

Happy	**Mad**	**Sad**
Scared	**Nervous**	**Guilty**
Excited	**Mixed Up**	**Loved**

GUESS WHICH CUP

Theme: Identifying and Coping with Feelings
Recommended Age Range: Six to Twelve
Treatment Modality: Individual
Stage of Treatment: Middle

Goals
• Facilitate open communication
• Encourage greater awareness of feelings
• Facilitate focusing and concentration skills

Materials
• Five paper cups
• Five slips of paper
• Bingo chips
• Prizes (see resource section)

Advance Preparation
On one of the five slips of paper, write Three Extra Chips. Write a feelings-related question on each of the four remaining paper slips. Some examples of feeling questions for younger children are:

> Show with your face and body what you look like when you feel happy.
> What makes you feel mad?
> What makes you feel sad?
> How would you feel if someone said something mean to you?

Some examples of feeling questions for older children are:

> What was the happiest day of your life?
> Name three things that make you feel mad.
> When was the last time you cried? What happened that made you so upset?
> What advice would you give to a child who was sad but pretended to be happy?

The questions can be modified to suit the age and treatment needs of each client. (For preschoolers, the game can be simplified by using three cups instead of five.) Next, fold the five strips of paper several times to form five small paper clumps. Place the paper cups on a table, (open end down) and place one paper clump under each cup.

Description

The therapist introduces the activity by stating:

We're going to play a game about feelings. Under each cup is a folded piece of paper. We're going to take turns moving the cups around (without lifting them up) and when the cups stop moving, one player chooses a cup, turns it over, unfolds the paper clump, reads aloud the question, and answers the question. The questions are all about feelings. If the player answers the question, he gets a chip. One of the cups is special and the player who picks it gets three extra chips. The game continues until all five cups have been picked. The chips are traded in at the end of the game for a prize.

Discussion

Open discussion of feelings is encouraged through this game. Focusing skills are also encouraged. This activity can be used again in later sessions with different questions, and the child can be encouraged to make up questions for the game.

Hint: The therapist may wish to place a discreet mark on the extra chips cup so the therapist knows not to pick that cup and the child then gets the extra chips.

GO FISH

Theme: Identifying and Coping with Feelings
Recommended Age Range: Six to Twelve
Treatment Modality: Individual, Small Group, Family
Stage of Treatment: Middle

Goals
• Encourage greater awareness of feelings
• Facilitate the healthy expression of feelings
• Increase feeling vocabulary

Materials
• Standard 52-card deck
• *Go Fish* sheet (included)
• Markers or crayons
• Scissors
• Glue
• Treats i.e., small candy, stickers, etc.

Advance Preparation
Make four copies of the *Go Fish* sheet. Cut out each square and glue the square onto the corresponding playing card. For example glue each Angry Ace onto an ace card from the stack of playing cards, glue each Terrible Two onto a number two card, glue Treat onto the Queen and King cards, glue Tell a Joke onto the Joker card, glue Do Ten Jumping Jacks onto the Jack cards, etc. (If this is too time consuming, an alternative is to photocopy the *Go Fish* sheet and use it as a guide while playing the *Go Fish* game.) Shuffle the deck of cards.

Description
This game is best for two to four players. The therapist begins by asking the children if they have ever played the card game, *Go Fish*. (Most children are familiar with the game and will respond to this question with enthusiasm.) The therapist states that they are going to play a special version of the *Go Fish* card game and explains the rules as follows:

The dealer deals five cards to each player (seven each for two players). The remaining cards are placed face down to form a stack. The player to the dealer's left starts. A turn consists of asking a player for a particular card. For example, if it is my turn I might say, "Do you have any Angry Aces?" The player who asks must already hold at least one card of the requested suit, so I must hold at least one Ace to say this. If the player who was asked has cards of the requested suit (Aces in this case), that player must hand over all his Aces to the player who asked for them. The asker then gets another turn and may again ask any player for any suit already in his or her hand. If the person asked does not have any cards of the requested suit, they say Go Fish! The asker must then draw the top card from the undealt stack. If the drawn card is the suit asked for, the asker shows it and gets another turn. If the drawn card is not the suit asked for, the asker keeps it, and the turn now passes to the player who said Go Fish! As soon as a player collects all four cards of the same suit (i.e., all four Angry Aces) this match must be shown to the other players. In order to win a point for that match, the player has to describe a time when he experienced that feeling (in this case, angry.) The player then places the four matched cards to his side, and the matches are counted at the end of the game. The game continues until either someone has no cards left in their hand or the stack runs out. The winner is the player who has the most matches.

Before the game begins, review the cards with the players. The numbered cards are feeling cards i.e., Angry Ace, Terrible Two, Thankful Three, Frustrated Four, Frightened Five, Sad Six, Surprised Seven, Excited Eight, Nervous Nine, and Terrific Ten. (If this activity is being used with younger children, explanations will likely be necessary for some of the feelings). The Jacks, Queens, Kings, and Jokers are special cards. If a player gets a match of Jacks, that player must do ten jumping jacks in order to win the point for that match. If a player gets a match of Queens or Kings, that player gets a treat, such as small candy, sticker, etc. If a player gets a match of Jokers, that player must tell a joke or make a funny face in order to win the point for that match.

Discussion

Most children are familiar with the *Go Fish* game and will enjoy this version. Some of the feeling words in the game will need to be explained, particularly if the activity is used with younger children. Once the children understand each of the feelings in the deck of cards, they are better able to ascribe feelings to situations in their own lives. As children talk about their feelings, the therapist can reflect their feelings, ask them to elaborate, and praise them for their openness. For example, the therapist can say, "I'm glad you felt comfortable enough talking about your sad feelings when your mom died. It took a lot of guts to share that so you really earned that point!" When it is the therapist's turn to share, the therapist can tailor his responses in a way that would be therapeutically beneficial to the child.

GO FISH SHEET

Angry Ace	Terrible Two	Thankful Three

Frustrated Four	Frightened Five	Sad Six

Surprised Seven	Excited Eight	Nervous Nine

Terrific Ten	Jumping Jack	Queen
	Do Ten Jumping Jacks!	

King	Joker
	Tell a Joke or Make a Funny Face

ANTI-STRESS KIT

Theme: Identifying and Coping with Feelings
Recommended Age Range: Ten and Up
Treatment Modality: Individual, Small Group
Stage of Treatment: Middle

Goals
• Identify signs of stress
• Assess the client using the stress questionnaire
• Promote healthy coping strategies

Materials
• One *Stress Questionnaire* for each client (included)
• Gift bag
• *Anti-Stress Kit Message Sheet* (included)
• Scissors
• Small self-adhesive dots

Advance Preparation
Copy one *Stress Questionnaire* and one *Anti-Stress Kit Message Sheet* for each client.

Description
Facilitate a discussion about stress and the meaning it has for the participants. The therapist can offer the following definition of stress: "Stress is created in the mind, and felt in the body, especially when people are feeling tired, worried, or pressured." The therapist and clients can share examples of times when they felt stressed out. Clients can also discuss or draw a picture of where they feel stress in their body. Clients then complete the *Stress Questionnaire* and discuss their responses.

Next, discuss ways to manage stress. The therapist can contribute to the discussion by offering ideas such as: accessing support, exercising, eating a healthy diet, releasing feelings of frustration, engaging in relaxing activities, and maintaining a sense of humor. The therapist then gives each client an *Anti-Stress Kit Message Sheet* and a gift bag. The clients choose which messages they want to cut out and put in their gift bags.

Lastly, discuss when and how the kit can be helpful. Clients take their kits home at the end of the session and can add their own ideas at a later time.

Discussion

This activity encourages clients to be proactive in reducing their stress level. Clients will enjoy the activity as they get to put their own *Anti-Stress Kits* together. During the activity, the therapist can point out that when people are feeling overly stressed, it is important to identify what is triggering the stress so they can eliminate the problem or cope with it more effectively. It should be emphasized that while some stressors cannot be eliminated, people can take steps to better manage their stress.

Some clients will need encouragement to use the strategies from their stress kits. One idea is for the therapist to help the client plan a Me Day. This may be sleeping in, then starting the day by eating a healthy breakfast, reading the comics section of the newspaper, watching a favorite movie, calling a friend, making up an exercise routine, then relaxing before bed by taking a hot bath and listening to soothing music.

STRESS QUESTIONNAIRE

Read the list below of possible stressors, and place a sticky dot on the ones that apply to you. You can put more dots on the items that are of greater concern to you.

1. I AM CONCERNED ABOUT DYING

2. I AM CONCERNED ABOUT MY HEALTH

3. I AM CONCERNED ABOUT MY SAFETY

4. I AM CONCERNED ABOUT MY FAMILY

5. I AM CONCERNED ABOUT MY APPEARANCE

6. I AM CONCERNED ABOUT MY SCHOOL WORK

7. I AM CONCERNED ABOUT FITTING IN WITH OTHERS

8. I AM CONCERNED ABOUT PEER PRESSURE

9. I AM CONCERNED ABOUT MY PAST

10. I AM CONCERNED ABOUT MY SEXUALITY

11. I AM CONCERNED ABOUT MONEY

12. I AM CONCERNED ABOUT THE ENVIRONMENT

13. I AM CONCERNED ABOUT GETTING INTO TROUBLE

14. I AM CONCERNED ABOUT VIOLENCE

15. I AM CONCERNED ABOUT MY FUTURE

ANTI-STRESS KIT MESSAGE SHEET

<table>
<tr>
<td>

I can <u>eat healthy</u>
to reduce my stress!

</td>
<td>

<u>Exercise</u> is a great
stress reliever! I can make
up an exercise routine, or
put on music and dance
around my room!

</td>
</tr>
<tr>
<td>

<u>Letting out my feelings</u> by
writing in my journal will
relieve my stress.

</td>
<td>

I can access <u>support</u> for
myself by talking to a
trusted friend, relative or
calling the crisis line.

</td>
</tr>
<tr>
<td>

<u>Laughter</u> is the best
medicine! I can read
the comics section
of the paper or watch a
funny movie.

</td>
<td>

I can <u>let out my
frustration</u> by
punching a pillow!

</td>
</tr>
<tr>
<td>

I can <u>ask for a hug</u>
to help myself feel better!

</td>
<td>

I can help myself feel
better by thinking of a
<u>happy memory.</u>

</td>
</tr>
<tr>
<td>

<u>Relaxation</u> will help me
feel better! I can listen
to relaxing music, read,
watch a movie, or
take a bath.

</td>
<td>

<u>Thinking positive</u> will
reduce my stress!
I can make a list of
positive thoughts.

</td>
</tr>
</table>

THEME SONG

Theme: Identifying and Coping with Feelings
Recommended Age Range: Twelve and Up
Treatment Modality: Individual, Group, Family
Stage of Treatment: Middle, End

Goals
• Facilitate positive coping strategies
• Encourage focus on positive feelings

Materials
• Tape or CD player

Description
The client is asked to bring a song to the session; one that has a positive message and is uplifting. The client plays the song for the therapist. At the end of the song, the therapist can ask questions such as, "What is your favorite part of the song?" and "How does this song make you feel?" The therapist encourages the client to play the song when she needs to be uplifted. The client may wish to write out their favorite verse from the song and post it in their bedroom.

Variation for group: Rather than having the participants play their whole songs, have them play their favorite part of the song.

Discussion
This activity was inspired by the television program, *Ally McBeal*. In this show, there is a comical scene between the main character, Ally, and her therapist, in which the therapist advises Ally to seek inspiration by choosing a theme song. This idea translates well to therapeutic work with adolescents, as adolescents typically respond well to music therapy. The activity empowers clients to make use of the healing powers of music.

CHAPTER THREE
ANGER MANAGEMENT

Children with anger management difficulties seem to represent a significantly higher number of referrals to counseling. Some children are referred to counseling because they are internalizing their anger, i.e. they are depressed or socially withdrawn. However, most referrals are of children who are externalizing their anger by acting out aggressively. Whether children internalize or externalize anger, they need to learn healthy ways to express and cope with their strong emotions. In this chapter, practical strategies are provided to help children recognize the signs of anger and develop better ways to cope and express their anger. In order for the anger management strategies to be most effective, children should be encouraged to practice newly learned skills outside the therapy session. Whenever possible, include parents in the counseling sessions, so they can learn the anger management techniques and coach children between sessions.

BRAINSTORMERS

Theme: Anger Management
Recommended Age Range: Nine and Up
Treatment Modality: Individual, Group
Stage of Treatment: Middle

Goals
• Facilitate open communication about anger
• Enhance anger management strategies

Materials
• Large pieces of paper or flip chart paper
• Markers
• *Brainstormers* list (included)
• Timer (i.e., watch, egg timer or sand timer)
• Prizes (see resource section for ideas)

Description
Divide the group into two teams. Explain the activity as follows:

We are going to play a brainstorming game that's going to help us talk about anger. The object of the game is for each team to come up with as many items as they can for each category. For example, if the category is 'things that make people laugh' then each team must make a list of things that make people laugh, and the team with the longest list wins that round. Each round lasts three minutes. At the end of each round, each team reads aloud the items on their list. If both teams have the same item on their lists, it gets crossed off. Each remaining item counts for one point. The points are accumulated each round, and the team with the most points at the end of the game wins.

Following the brainstorming activity, the therapist can facilitate a discussion by asking the following questions:

> What did you learn about anger?
> Why is it important to learn safe ways to express anger?
> Which anger management strategies work best for you?

Variation for individual therapy: The child brainstorms on his own and is awarded points for each item on the list. The points can be accumulated and traded in at the end for a prize.

Discussion

This is a useful introductory activity to do at the beginning of an anger management curriculum as it helps clients begin to discuss issues related to anger. This activity promotes communication, catharsis of feelings, and problem solving. The brainstorming format encourages creative thinking and open dialogue about anger-related issues. The reward system motivates clients and adds an element of fun to the activity.

BRAINSTORMERS

Things that make kids your age angry

Things that make adults angry

Other words for "angry" (Swear words are not allowed!)

Things that happen to your body when you feel angry

Unsafe ways to express anger

Ways to help your body relax when you feel angry

People kids can talk to when they feel angry

Negative things kids say to themselves that make them feel angrier

Positive messages you can say to yourself to calm yourself down when you feel angry

IF YOU'RE MAD AND YOU KNOW IT

Theme: Anger Management
Recommended Age Range: Four to Six
Treatment Modality: Individual, Small and Large Group, Family
Stage of Treatment: Middle

Goals
• Raise understanding that certain expressions of anger are unacceptable
• Facilitate appropriate expression of anger

Materials
• *Okay and Not Okay Ways to Show Mad Feelings* guide (included)
• *If You're Mad And You Know It* Song sheet (included)
• Full length mirror (optional)

Description
There are three parts to this activity. The first part helps children identify their mad feelings. Part two teaches children anger management techniques. The last part is a music and movement activity to facilitate skill rehearsal and integration.

Begin by asking the children to identify what makes them feel mad (they can verbalize or draw a picture.) Next, ask the children to show with their face and body what they look like when they are feeling mad. (The therapist and children can have a mad face contest!) The therapist then reviews the *Okay and Not Okay Ways to Show Mad Feelings* guide with the children. Each *Okay Ways to Show Mad Feelings* technique is demonstrated and practiced. If desired, the children can take turns standing in front of a mirror to practice the techniques. They can also practice the techniques by enacting the following role plays:

> You are at the store and your mom won't buy you a treat. Instead of throwing a tantrum, you do the turtle.

> You are playing a computer game and you get mad because you are losing. Instead of screaming out loud, you do a silent scream.

> You get sent to your room for bugging your sister. You calm yourself down by doing the ragdoll.

> You feel mad when another kid calls you stupid. Instead of being mean back, you walk away.

As a closing activity, the therapist leads the children in the song, *If You're Mad And You Know It* (this is an adapted version of the song, *If You're Mad and You Know It Clap Your Hands*).

Discussion

This activity involves psychoeducation as well as music and movement. It helps young children identify anger and learn appropriate anger management techniques. Rehearsing learned skills is encouraged through the role plays and the song. Song sheets can be distributed to parents so they can help their children practice the new anger management strategies at home. Encourage parents to praise their children whenever they use the new anger management strategies.

OKAY AND NOT OKAY WAYS
TO SHOW MAD FEELINGS

NOT OKAY	OKAY
Hurting someone with your body	Turtle technique
Hurting someone with words	Silent scream
Throwing a tantrum	Robot/rag doll
Breaking something	Walk away

Turtle technique: In a standing position, pull head in toward body.

Silent scream: Use face and body gestures to scream without any noise coming out.

Robot/rag doll: Tighten body muscles like a robot then loosen your muscles like a rag doll.

Walk away: Face forward then turn around and walk away.

Song Sheet
IF YOU'RE MAD AND YOU KNOW IT

(Sung to the tune of, *If You're Happy And You Know It Clap Your Hands*)

If you're mad and you know it do the turtle
If you're mad and you know it do the turtle
If you're mad and you know it
And you really want to show it
If you're mad and you know it do the turtle!

If you're mad and you know it do a silent scream
If you're mad and you know it do a silent scream
If you're mad and you know it
And you really want to show it
If you're mad and you know it do a silent scream!

If you're mad and you know it do the rag doll
If you're mad and you know it do the rag doll
If you're mad and you know it
And you really want to show it
If you're mad and you know it do the rag doll!

If you're mad and you know it walk away
If you're mad and you know it walk away
If you're mad and you know it
And you really want to show it
If you're mad and you know it walk away!

ANGER WORKBOOK

Theme: Anger Management
Recommended Age Range: Nine and Up
Treatment Modality: Individual, Small Group, Family
Stage of Treatment: Middle

Goals
• Facilitate open communication about anger
• Enhance anger management strategies

Materials
• One *Anger Workbook* for each client (included)
• Markers

Advance Preparation
Make a copy of the *Anger Workbook* for each client.

Description
The therapist introduces the activity by stating they are going to do an activity about angry feelings. The child is then provided with the *Anger Workbook* to complete. The child begins by decorating the cover of the workbook, then completes the remaining pages. (If this activity is used with younger children, the therapist can read and transcribe the child's answers.) The child's responses and drawings are discussed as the child completes the workbook. The homework sheet is given to the child at the end of the session to complete, and reviewed in the next session. (**Note:** This activity is best completed over several sessions.)

Discussion
Many children have difficulty controlling their anger. These children may not know how to control strong emotions. If these children do not learn how to better manage their anger, it can lead to ongoing personal and social problems. This activity will help children express their anger, learn strategies for self-control, and provide opportunities for skill rehearsal.

Caregiver involvement in the child's treatment is always encouraged, and in particular they should help the child with the homework component of this activity. Meeting with caregivers to help them model anger control skills is also helpful.

_____'S

ANGER WORKBOOK

Hi! This is a book about angry feelings. But before we talk about angry feelings, let's get to know you. Fill in an answer for each of the questions below:

I am _____ years old.

When I'm not in school I like to _____

I think it's cool when _____

I laugh about _____

I cry about _____

I love it when _____

I hate it when _____

I think _____

My family is _____

Kids at school _____

I am good at _____

I wish _____

I am working on _____

Now that we know you better, let's talk about angry feelings. Anger is a normal emotion. Everyone gets angry sometimes. Draw a picture of something that makes you feel angry:

Sometimes people lose their temper when they get angry, and they do things that get them into trouble. Some people lose their temper with words (call names, tease, yell, swear, threaten) and some people lose their temper with their body (slam doors, throw things, punch walls, bang head, push, bite, kick, hit). Draw a picture of a time you got into trouble after losing your temper:

Draw a picture to show how you felt when you got into trouble for losing your temper:

Draw a picture to show how you feel when you're not in trouble:

You can learn better ways to handle your anger so you can stay out of trouble and feel better about yourself. Check off on the list below the ideas you would like to try:

___ Slowly count backwards

___ Breathing (breathe in for four seconds, hold it four seconds, let it out four seconds)

___ Ignore the person

___ Walk away

___ Talk to an adult about my feelings

___ Visualize a STOP sign

___ Say to myself, "Chill out!"

___ Do the turtle (pull head in toward body)

___ Robot/ragdoll (tighten muscles like a robot then loosen muscles like a ragdoll)

___ Think of a time I handled my anger well to remind myself I can do it

___ Remind myself how badly I feel when I get in trouble for losing my temper

Other ideas: _____

Choose one of the ideas from the previous page and draw a picture of a situation when you can use that idea:

Draw a picture giving yourself a pat on the back for learning new ways to handle your anger:

Now that you've learned some better ways to handle your anger, it's time to practice. Choose one of the ideas that you learned about today to practice this week. Fill in the contract below:

This week, when I get angry, I will try to handle my anger by:

_____

Fill in the homework sheet on the next page and bring it to your next session.

HANDLING MY ANGER HOMEWORK SHEET

Situation that made me feel angry (draw or write what happened)

Check off what happened when you got angry:

__Didn't try to handle my anger better at all

__Handled my anger better by _____

ROAD RAGE

Theme: Anger Management
Recommended Age Range: Seven to Twelve
Treatment Modality: Individual, Small Group, Family
Stage of Treatment: Middle

Goals
• Normalize angry feelings
• Facilitate appropriate expression of anger
• Develop problem-solving skills

Materials
• *Road Rage* game board (included)
• Red, yellow, and green card stock or card board
• Hershey's Chocolate Hugs®
• Blow horns
• Car stickers
• Toy car
• Snacks for Pit Stop
• Two bags
• *Road Rage Cards* (included)

Advance Preparation
Obtain permission from caregivers to offer snacks.
Photocopy and enlarge the game board, and if desired, laminate it for extra durability.
(Tip: Use an old game board and glue this game onto it.) Color the traffic lights on the game board the appropriate color (i.e.) The first square after Start should be colored green, the second square is red, the third square is yellow, etc. Photocopy the *Road Rage* cards onto the red, green and yellow card stock or copy the cards onto colored cardboard. Place the Hershey's Chocolate Hugs®, blow horns, and car stickers in a bag, which is kept by the therapist's side. Place the snacks in another bag. Set up the game board as follows:

1. Place the toy car on the space marked Start.
2. Place the three sets of game cards beside the game board.
3. Place the bag with the snacks in the space marked Pit Stop on the game board.

Description
The therapist introduces the activity by indicating they are going to play a game called *Road Rage* that will help teach ways to express anger. The game is explained as follows:

Players take turns moving the toy car along the game path from the Start space to the space marked End of the Journey. Players follow the directions as they land on the game board squares. When players land on the spaces with the traffic lights, they pick a corresponding question card and follow the directions:
Red light = Red cards: <u>Stop</u> to practice an anger management technique.
Yellow light = Yellow cards: <u>Slow down</u> to ask the group a true or false question.
Green light = Green cards: <u>Go</u> get a treat from the treat bag.

When players land on the square marked Pit Stop they distribute snacks to all the drivers. The game continues until the players reach the End of the Journey and they honk their horns!

At the end of the game, the therapist has the children identify one technique they can use to cope with their anger.

Discussion

Many children have difficulty expressing their anger appropriately so it is important to provide children with opportunities to learn ways to manage their anger within a safe therapeutic environment. Within the context of the *Road Rage* game, children learn, practice, and integrate anger management skills. The Green Treat Cards and Pit Stop snacks are included to add appeal to the activity and to maintain the children's interest in the game.

Note: The green treat cards should be stacked in the following order:
1. Chocolate hugs
2. Car stickers
3. Blowhorns

ROAD RAGE CARDS

RED CARDS (Copy onto red card board)   **YELLOW CARDS** (Copy onto yellow card board)

<u>Stop to practice a new technique</u>
You missed the stop sign!
Practice visualizing a stop
sign as a reminder to
Stop and Think.

<u>Slow down to answer a question</u>
True or False: Anger is a bad emotion.
False: Anger is a normal emotion;
everyone gets angry sometimes.

<u>Stop to practice a new technique</u>
A police officer pulls you over
for reckless driving.
Practice taking responsibility
for your mistakes by apologizing.

<u>Slow down to answer a question</u>
True or false: Your body changes
when you are angry.
True: When you are angry your
muscles tighten, you breathe faster, and
your heart rate speeds up.

<u>Stop to practice a new technique</u>
You got caught speeding!
Practice walking around the
room in slow motion to remind
yourself to take it slow.

<u>Slow down to answer a question</u>
True or False: If I ignore my angry
feelings I will feel better.
False: If you do not deal with your
anger, it will build and make you feel
more tense and upset.

<u>Stop to practice a new technique</u>
Another car cut you off!
Practice counting back-
wards from twenty to
help yourself calm down.

<u>Slow down to answer a question</u>
True or false: Kids who express their
anger inappropriately are bad.
False: Just because kids behave
inappropriately doesn't mean
they are bad.

<u>Stop to practice a new technique</u>
You are stuck in a traffic jam
and feel frustrated and impatient.
Practice deep breathing to help
yourself relax.

<u>Slow down to answer a question</u>
True or False: When you feel angry
it is helpful to play basketball.
True: Exercise is a great way to calm
down. Once you are calm you can deal
with your anger.

GREEN CARDS (Copy onto greed card board)

<u>Go get a treat!</u>
Some bumpy roads ahead.
Give each driver a chocolate
hug to help brace for the ride.

<u>Go get a treat!</u>
You are driving along the
road to recovery.
Give each driver a car sticker.

<u>Go get a treat!</u>
You reached the end of
your journey! Give each player a
blow-horn, and blow your horns to show
how proud you are for a job well done!

ROAD RAGE!

START →

End of the Journey

PIT STOP

PIT STOP

RATE IT

Theme: Anger Management
Recommended Age Range: Nine and Up
Treatment Modality: Individual, Group, Family
Stage of Treatment: Middle

Goals
• Encourage exploration of appropriate expressions of anger
• Assess judgment and coping skills
• Enhance problem-solving skills

Materials
• *Rate It!* cards (included)
• One *Rate Yourself* homework sheet for each client (included)

Advance Preparation
Photocopy the *Rate It!* cards onto colored card stock and cut out each card, or copy each scenario onto a separate index card.

Description
Distribute the *Rate It!* cards to the client. The client completes the cards by reading each scenario, ranking the person's decision, explaining the reason for the ranking, and describing other more appropriate ways for handling the situation. The scenarios are then discussed. If this activity is done in a group, the members are encouraged to discuss and debate peer responses. Clients can then create their own scenarios by using the blank cards.

A variation of the activity is for the group members to role-play the scenarios then brainstorm more positive or adaptive solutions.

The homework sheet should be reviewed prior to the end of the session and discussed in the following session.

Discussion
This activity enables clients to enhance problem solving and anger management skills so they are better equipped to deal with anger-provoking situations. The homework assignment enables clients to self-monitor and evaluate their own behavior, which leads to greater awareness and mastery of anger management skills.

RATE IT!

SITUATION

Rob is standing in line at the movie theater to buy tickets. Another boy cuts in front of him in line. Rob calmly tells the boy he was ahead in line and it is rude to cut in.

DECISION
Good   Fair   Poor

REASON

If it was a poor decision, write a better alternative

SITUATION

Tisha found out that her sister took her favorite CD without asking and lost it at school. Tisha decided to get back at her sister by dumping all of her sister's CD's into the bathtub.

DECISION
Good   Fair   Poor

REASON

If it was a poor decision, write a better alternative

SITUATION

Ricardo's teacher catches him talking in class and warns him to stop or he will get a detention. Ricardo becomes angry and swears at the teacher.

DECISION
Good   Fair   Poor

REASON

If it was a poor decision, write a better alternative

SITUATION

Eva asks her mother if she can go to the mall with some friends. Her mother says no because she did not finish her chores. Eva negotiates with her mother to go to the mall once she has done her chores.

DECISION
Good   Fair   Poor

REASON

If it was a poor decision, write a better alternative

SITUATION

Pina does poorly on a test at school. A girl in her class sees her test results and calls her stupid. Pina responds by punching the other girl.

DECISION
Good   Fair   Poor

REASON

If it was a poor decision, write a better alternative

SITUATION

Ari is playing a computer game. He becomes frustrated because he is not doing well in the game. He takes three deep breaths to help himself calm down.

DECISION
Good   Fair   Poor

REASON

If it was a poor decision, write a better alternative

SITUATION

Vince found out that his girlfriend kissed another guy. He became enraged and hit his girlfriend.

DECISION
Good   Fair   Poor

REASON

If it was a poor decision, write a better alternative

SITUATION

Debra's parents are divorced. She becomes upset when her father does not show up for a scheduled visit. She barricades herself in the bathroom and forces herself to vomit.

DECISION
Good   Fair   Poor

REASON

If it was a poor decision, write a better alternative

Homework Sheet
RATE YOURSELF

SITUATION

DECISION

Good   Fair   Poor

REASON

If it was a poor decision, write a better alternative:

SITUATION

DECISION

Good   Fair   Poor

REASON

If it was a poor decision, write a better alternative:

SITUATION

DECISION

Good   Fair   Poor

REASON

If it was a poor decision, write a better alternative:

SITUATION

DECISION

Good   Fair   Poor

REASON

If it was a poor decision, write a better alternative:

DON'T FLIP YOUR LID
A SIX-WEEK ANGER MANAGEMENT PROGRAM

Theme: Anger Management
Recommended Age Range: Seven to Twelve
Treatment Modality: Individual, Small Group
Stage of Treatment: Middle

Goals
• Facilitate open communication about anger
• Enhance anger management strategies

Materials
• One box with a lid for each client (i.e., plastic container, shoe box, or insulated lunch bag)
• Self-adhesive labels
• Props (select four from the list of *Anger Management Techniques and Props*)
• Five *Don't Flip Your Lid* homework sheets for each client (included)

Advance Preparation
Make five copies of the homework sheet for each client.

Description
This activity works best as a six-week program as outlined below.

Session one: Introduction of the program and identification of angry feelings
Introduce the *Don't Flip Your Lid* anger management program by asking the child to define the expression, Don't Flip Your Lid. If the child is unfamiliar with the expression, the therapist can offer an explanation such as:

When someone says 'don't flip your lid' it means don't lose control or freak out when you get mad. This program is called Don't Flip Your Lid because it teaches kids new ways of dealing with angry feelings so they don't flip their lids when they get angry. You get your own flip box and each week you will learn a new anger management technique and you will receive a prop to put in your box that will help you remember to practice that technique.

Next, ask the child, "What makes you flip your lid?" Provide the child with self-adhesive labels on which he writes what makes him angry. If the child has difficulty identifying angry thoughts and feelings, the therapist can ask prompt questions such as:
     What makes kids your age angry?
     What is something about your family that makes you angry?
     What is something about school that makes you angry?

The child sticks the labels on the inside of the box lid. The child can then decorate the outside of the box.

For homework, the child is provided with self-adhesive labels to take home and he is asked to write on the labels anything that happens during the week that makes him angry. The labels are brought back to the next session and added to the child's flip box.

The child completes the homework sheet and signs it (younger children will need assistance completing the sheet). Ideally, the child's caregivers will be included and can sign the homework sheet as well. The child completes the second part of the homework sheet at home and it is reviewed at the beginning of the next session.

Sessions two to five: Anger management strategies

The therapist selects four anger management techniques from the list provided, and teaches the child a new technique each session. Each technique has a prop that the child adds to his flip box. The child can take the flip box home between sessions and use the prop as a reminder to practice the anger management technique.

Session six: Consolidation and graduation

In this last session, the child is asked to identify which anger management technique he found most effective. The child is encouraged to use this technique whenever he becomes angry. The child's progress is reviewed and celebrated.

Discussion

Children generally respond well to this anger management program, as it is engaging and concrete. The props encourage opportunities for skill rehearsal so that the techniques can be better integrated into the child's repertoire. The client can complete the homework sheet independently or with guidance from a caregiver. Self-evaluation is encouraged by asking the child in follow-up sessions to identify when he used a particular technique and how effective it was in helping him to manage his anger. For example, the child can be asked to give examples of when he used the technique and whether the technique helped a little, a lot, or not at all. Ultimately, the goal is to enable the client to apply the anger management strategies to real-life situations.

Caregiver involvement will enhance the effectiveness of this anger management program. Caregivers can be taught the techniques so they can model their use and coach their children. Caregivers should also be encouraged to provide positive reinforcement by praising the child when he uses appropriate anger management strategies.

Anger Management
TECHNIQUES AND PROPS

Anger Management Techniques	Props
Turtle technique (pull head in toward body)	Miniature turtle, turtle sticker, or drawing of turtle
Count backwards	Sand timer, or written direction that reads: Count backwards from 25
Get a grip	Tension ball or written direction that reads: Tense then relax your fists
Exercise	Skipping rope or written direction that reads: Do ten jumping jacks
Four Breathing (breathe in for four seconds, hold breath for four seconds, let it out for four seconds)	A picture of the number four
Say and think STOP!	Photo or drawing of a stop sign
Tell yourself to chill out!	Ice pack or written direction that reads: Chill out!
Visualize a proud moment	Memento or written description of a personal achievement
Have a seat (sitting down causes the body to relax)	Chair from doll house set or written direction that reads: Have a seat
Chew gum (this repetitive motion helps self-soothe)	Gum

HOMEWORK
DON'T FLIP YOUR LID

(Fill in this section at the end of the session)

Today I learned to handle my anger by: _____

My prop will help me remember to: _____

I can practice this technique at home by: _____

My caregiver can help me practice by: _____

Child's signature: _____

Caregiver's signature: _____

Therapist's signature: _____

• •

(Fill in this section at home and bring it to your next session)

Situation that made me angry: _____

Anger management technique used: _____

How this technique helped me: _____

How my caregiver helped me: _____

CHAPTER FOUR
SOCIAL SKILLS

Many troubled children and youth are socially immature and antisocial. They lack basic social skills, and as a result, they are often alienated from their peers. Learning to relate appropriately to others, therefore, is an important treatment goal for many children referred for counseling. The socialization games and activities in this chapter can be incorporated into a social skills curriculum to help children master a variety of social behaviors, such as forming and maintaining healthy friendships, communicating effectively, cooperating with others, and being assertive. As would be expected, socialization activities are most appropriate for use in group counseling settings, so children can learn, practice and rehearse prosocial behaviors. The therapist can observe the group dynamics and provide constructive feedback to children on how they relate to others. Children can also gain insight into their behavior by accepting feedback from their peers. It is recommended that the therapist join in on the activities in order to model positive social behavior.

BUBBLES

Theme: Social Skills
Recommended Age Range: Four to Six
Treatment Modality: Small Group
Stage of Treatment: Middle

Goals
• Acquire awareness of socially acceptable behavior
• Provide opportunity for skill rehearsal

Materials
• Bubbles

Description
Group members stand in a circle. The leader explains the activity as follows:

These bubbles are going to be passed around the group. Each of you will have a turn to blow bubbles three times as long as you follow the rules. There are four rules:

1) Wait your turn
2) Say, "Please may I play with the bubbles" when it is your turn
3) Say, "Thank you for giving me the bubbles" when you are given the bubbles
4) Share the bubbles by passing them to the next person when your turn is over

If you break any of these rules, you miss your turn. Let's see if we can all play the game by following the rules.

Before commencing the activity have the children repeat the four rules to ensure they understand the expectations.

The bubbles are passed around the group twice. As the bubbles are passed around, the leader facilitates by reminding the children of the four rules: to wait their turn, say please, thank you, and to share. The leader praises the children by making comments such as,

I like how you are waiting patiently for your turn
It's nice to hear you say please and thank you
You know how to share

(**Note:** The therapist may wish to hold the bubble jar while the children dip the wand to avoid spills.)

Following the bubble activity, the therapist can facilitate a discussion about what was learned. Skills can be generalized to outside the group by discussing examples such as, if you are playing in the sand box at the playground and you want to borrow someone's shovel, what can you say?

Discussion

This activity facilitates prosocial behavior by enabling children to practice skills such as self-control and communication. The group format provides an excellent environment for children to rehearse social skills and gain immediate peer feedback. The combination of the group play, followed by the discussion, enables children to integrate the skills. A token economy system can be used to encourage positive behavior.

KERPLUNK®

Theme: Social Skills
Recommended Age Range: Seven to Twelve
Treatment Modality: Individual, Small Group
Stage of Treatment: Middle

Goals
• Develop prosocial behavior
• Provide opportunity for skill rehearsal

Materials
• *Kerplunk!*® game (available in the board game section of toy stores)
• *Kerplunk!*® question cards (included)
• Index cards or card stock
• Large sheet of paper
• Thick marker
• Tape

Advance Preparation
Copy each question from the *Kerplunk!*® question card sheet onto separate index cards, or photocopy the question card sheet onto card stock and cut out each question.

Description
The leader asks if anyone has ever played the game, *Kerplunk!*®. Many children will be familiar with the game and will respond with enthusiasm. The leader states that the group is going to play a special version of the *Kerplunk!*® game. The leader reads the instructions that come with the *Kerplunk!*® game, and then indicates that the group is going to follow these rules, but if any marbles fall during a player's turn, the group yells, KERPLUNK! and that player must answer one of the questions.

Next, the leader explains the need for special safety rules: "This game comes with sharp plastic sticks and hard marbles. The game would be no fun if someone got hurt, so before we begin, let's make up some group rules so this game is fun and safe for everyone in the group." Each group member then identifies a rule, and the rule is written on the large sheet of paper taped to the wall. The rules are reviewed before the game begins. If a group member breaks a rule during the game, the leader stops the game, and reminds the group of the rules. Another option is to have rule cards (see Child Management Techniques in the Appendix.)

Discussion

This activity provides children with an opportunity to enhance their ego-strengths, using the game of *Kerplunk!*® as an engaging tool. Through this game format, various issues are addressed such as, impulse control, frustration tolerance, and feelings of competition.

During the activity, the leader can take advantage of teachable moments by intervening if children act out. For example, if a child becomes aggressive during the game, the leader can say, "It's important everyone follow the rule about no hurts so this game can be safe and fun for everyone." At the end of the game, the group leader can ask the children for examples of how they can apply the skills learned in this session to situations outside the therapy setting.

Questions
KERPLUNK®

-1-
KERPLUNK!
It's important to play by the rules, even if it means losing the game. How would you feel if someone else were not playing by the rules?

-2-
KERPLUNK!
We all hate to lose so sometimes we cheat in order to win the game. Role-play an appropriate way to handle cheating.

-3-
KERPLUNK!
This game is fun! Sometimes we are having so much fun playing that we forget to wait our turn. How do you feel when someone doesn't wait their turn during a game?

-4-
KERPLUNK!
This game can feel frustrating sometimes! Help the group come up with three ideas on how to deal with frustration.

-5-
KERPLUNK!
Sometimes kids lose their cool when they lose and start a fight. Help the group identify three ways to stay calm.

-6-
KERPLUNK!
Things don't always go your way. Tell about a time when things didn't go your way.

-7-
KERPLUNK!
Kids can be mean sometimes and tease you when you lose a game. Role-play an appropriate way to handle teasing.

-8-
KERPLUNK!
"If all the marbles fall, you lose it all!" What can you say to yourself so you don't feel bad when you lose a game?

THE GETTING ALONG WITH OTHERS GAME

Theme: Social Skills
Recommended Age Range: Seven and Up
Treatment Modality: Individual, Small Group, Family
Stage of Treatment: Middle

Goals
• Develop active listening skills, effective communication, and assertive behavior
• Provide opportunities for skill rehearsal

Materials
• Six envelopes (or enough for all players, including the group leader, to have a turn)
• One small prize and one large prize (see resource section for ideas)
• *Getting Along With Others* questions (included)
• Poster board

Advance Preparation
If the treats are a food item obtain permission from caregivers to offer food.

Write the following in large bold letters at the top of a large piece of poster board:
The Getting Along With Others Game. Tape the board to the wall. Tape the envelopes to the board. Photocopy the question sheet and cut out and fold each question. Place each question in a separate envelope on the game board. (Note: The questions can be adapted to suit the age and treatment needs of the group members.)

Description
Explain the game as follows:

Players take turns pulling a card from one of the envelopes. When a player selects a question card, that player reads the question aloud and answers it. All the questions have to do with getting along with others. If a player gets a prize card, that player gets a prize. The game continues until all the envelopes are empty. All players who participate actively get to share a prize at the end of the game.

Variation for individual therapy: Same as above, except the therapist and child take turns selecting question cards.

Discussion

This activity provides children with an opportunity to strengthen their social skills, using the game format as an engaging tool. Through the game format, children develop important social skills such as, starting a conversation, making eye contact, listening, being assertive, dealing with bullies, compromising, and giving compliments.

To generalize the skills learned, the therapist can ask the group for examples of how they can apply what they learned in the session to situations outside the therapy setting.

Questions
GETTING ALONG WITH OTHERS

It can be hard to start a conversation with people you do not know well. Pretend you are invited to a birthday party and you don't know anybody, except the person who invited you. Practice going up to someone and starting a conversation. Have a one-minute conversation.

It is important to listen when someone is talking. Practice your listening skills by having someone in the group talk to you for one-minute, then summarize what that person said.

You can learn to be assertive (standing up for yourself in a respectful, non-violent way). Practice being assertive in the following situation: Someone tells you your friend is spreading rumors about you.

It hurts to be bullied but you can do something about it. Practice asserting yourself in the following situation: You are walking down the hall and another kid trips you on purpose, then laughs at you.

It is important to make and keep eye contact when someone is talking to you. Practice having a conversation with someone and keep eye contact for one-minute.

It feels good to receive compliments. Give a compliment to each person in the group.

Compromising means giving up something in order to reach an agreement. Tell about a time you compromised.

PRIZE!

PARTICIPATION: A STORY ABOUT BULLYING

Theme: Social Skills
Recommended Age Range: Seven to Twelve
Treatment Modality: Individual, Small and Large Group
Stage of Treatment: Middle

Goals
• Facilitate communication about bullying
• Enhance problem-solving skills with regard to bullying
• Build empathy so children will be more sensitive toward those who are bullied

Materials
• *Participaction* story (included)

Description
The therapist introduces the activity by stating:

I am going to read a story. When you hear a feeling word in the story you must mime that feeling without making any sounds. For example, if the story is: "The boy was very **Excited** *as he opened his birthday presents, but then he felt* **Disappointed** *because he did not get the computer game he really wanted" then you would mime being excited, then being disappointed. Let's practice miming the feelings.*

The therapist then reads aloud each feeling below, and the children mime the feelings:

Excited
Nervous
Relieved
Embarrassed
Lonely
Scared
Jealous
Confused
Angry
Shy
Happy
Worried
Hurt
Confident
Surprised

The therapist then explains that the story is about bullying and it is important to listen carefully because there is an activity about the story afterward. The children stand and mime the feelings as the story is read aloud. The story is then processed. Discussion questions include:

Bullies often pick on others in order to get attention or gain power and control. Sometimes bullies are or were bullied themselves at home or in some other situation. Identify more appropriate ways for kids to meet their needs for attention, power, and control.

Kids get teased or bullied because they appear to be easy targets and they have difficulty standing up for themselves. Identify appropriate ways for kids to stand up for themselves.

It hurts to be teased or bullied because kids believe what the bully says instead of believing in themselves and their own abilities. Make a list of your positive qualities and abilities and keep this list handy so you can look at it next time you are teased.

Everyone plays a role in bullying. What role do you play? (bully, victim, or bystander?) What can you do to stop bullying at your school or in your neighborhood? (i.e., Start a Bully Watch program or develop a Bill of Rights for your classroom.)

As an optional activity, the children can draw pictures or make up role-plays about the anti-bullying techniques learned through the story.

Discussion

Bullying is, unfortunately, an all too common problem. Many anti-bullying programs are now being used in schools. This activity can be used as part of an anti-bullying program. It develops sensitivity to the issue of bullying and provides practical strategies to deal more effectively with bullying. The *Participaction* story maintains children's interest as they listen for the feelings then act them out.

As a variation with larger groups, the children can be divided into subgroups and each group can be assigned a different feeling to mime.

PARTICIPACTION: A STORY ABOUT BULLLYING

Sam dragged his swim bag out of the back seat of the car and slammed the door. His mom rolled down the window and gave him a reassuring smile. "Have fun at swim lessons, honey! I'll pick you up at two o'clock."

Sam stared at the ground and felt that **nervous** knot in his stomach tighten as he trudged slowly toward the building. As he entered the boys locker room, he looked around and felt **relieved** to find it empty. *Maybe those mean kids aren't even here this year, so why feel so **worried**?* Sam opened his locker and discovered a mysterious pink package inside. His heart sank, and he felt **scared**. *It looks like Michael, Nathan, and Chris are back and up to their old tricks.* Sam heard snickering as footsteps entered the locker room.

"Welcome back Pee Wee! Hope you don't mind but we got tired of you peeing in the pool last year so we bought you a stack of baby swim diapers. We figured girls size small should fit just about right!" Their laughter erupted.

"OK boys, come on out! We're about to start," came a Coach's voice from just outside. Sam heard a loud crack and felt a stinging pain strike the backs of his legs as Michael, Nathan, and Chris snapped their towels in unison.

The boys shouted over their shoulders, "See you in the pool, Pee Wee!"

Feeling **hurt, angry** and **embarrassed**, Sam slouched on the bench beside his locker, massaging his legs. He fought back tears and **worried** how he would make it through the day.

At lunch time Sam hurried out of the water and found an empty bench. He felt **lonely** and **jealous** of the other kids roaming about laughing, chatting, and eating their lunches in large groups. Sam noticed someone walking toward him. He felt scared and his heart began to pound. Sam kept his head down. As the person drew nearer, he relaxed.

It's just that older kid Gina... I wonder what she wants?

Gina stopped in front of Sam and held out a paper bag.

"I found this lunch bag with your name on it and thought you might be wondering where it was."

Gina smiled kindly and Sam slowly took the bag from her hands. **Confused**, Sam barely mumbled "thanks" as Gina turned to walk back towards her friends on the other side of the pool.

What was she talking about? I didn't bring my lunch here in a paper bag.

Sam carefully unraveled the top and looked inside. He pulled out a small plastic baggy full of dog biscuits and flushed deep red as he saw a note pinned to the bag. It read *'Hope these biscuits help you improve your doggy paddle this year!'* A roar of laughter rose up from a group of boys sitting at the edge of the pool. Certain that *everyone* was staring and laughing at him, Sam stuffed the dog biscuits back into the bag and stumbled towards the boys locker room. Feeling **angry** and **embarrassed**, Sam threw the paper bag in the trash can and kicked it with his foot. *I can't go back out there! Maybe I can just pretend I'm sick and call my mom to come and pick me up early.*

"Sam... are you in there? It's Gina... I need to talk to you."

"What do you want?"

"Look, I just heard what happened and I want you to know I had nothing to do with that prank those bullies pulled. I just thought I was bringing you your lunch. I'm really sorry!" Sam could barely believe what he was hearing.

"Look, I have to get back to practice, but let's meet at the end of the day so we can talk about this. I think I might be able to help you."

Sam hesitated, hardly knowing what to think. "Well... okay... I guess so."

Later, feeling **relieved** that swim practice was finally over, Sam met Gina on the bench outside the locker rooms. "You know, they only pick on you because you look like an easy target to them," Gina began. "Those bullies can tell in a second that you're a good victim just by the way you walk around the pool."

"What do you mean?"

"Well, you're always staring at the floor, like you're **scared** to look up at anyone," Gina explained. "And you mumble and speak so softly that you don't give people a chance to get to know you."

"But it seems like everyone hates me! If I look up I'm **worried** I'll just get teased even more."

"That's where you're wrong," said Gina. "I was a lot like you when I started swimming three years ago. I felt really **shy**, and I didn't like being seen in a bathing suit. Some of the other girls whispered about me and giggled whenever I came into the locker room. I was **scared** going to lessons and I almost quit. But then I decided to just pretend that the teasing didn't bother me and I started holding my head up high. I call it my Winner's Walk. You have to look like a winner to feel like one."

"It can't be that easy," said Sam

"Well, I also came up with a few good comebacks, which I used whenever they said anything mean to me." Gina went on. "This really **surprised** them because they thought I was too quiet and meek to say anything at all. After a while some of the nicer girls began talking to me and the mean ones realized their teasing wasn't getting anywhere so they just stopped!" Now I have more friends, and I feel **happy** and more **confident**."

"What kinds of things did you say to them when they teased you?"

"One good one is, 'I feel sorry for you having to get your kicks by hurting other people,'" said Gina. "Or you could say, 'I'm not going to let you bug me'. And then just walk away."

"I don't know..." sighed Sam. "It's hard to imagine even being able to look at those guys let alone keep my head up high."

"I know it's not easy. But try to think of one thing you're proud of or feel good about, then keep thinking about that thing while you keep your head up. It's important to feel **confident**."

"Well... I'm actually a pretty good tennis player," Sam admitted.

"That's great! Next time those boys start teasing you about being last to finish laps, you should ask them if they'd like to come and play a game of tennis with you!"

Sam laughed and realized how good it felt. He felt **happy** and **relieved** that the knot in his stomach was finally gone. "Thanks Gina. I think I'm going to practice some comebacks and that Winner Walk when I get home." Sam saw his mother turn the car into the parking lot and he smiled, realizing he felt **excited** to come back for the next day's swim lesson!

(Story by Jennifer Meader)

MVP (MOST VALUABLE PLAYER)

Theme: Social Skills
Recommended Age Range: Seven and Up
Treatment Modality: Small and Large Group
Stage of Treatment: Middle

Goals
- Facilitate awareness of appropriate social skills
- Reward pro-social behavior
- Encourage positive peer feedback

Materials
- Score sheet (included)
- *Certificate of Achievement* (included)
- Card stock

Advance Preparation
Photocopy the *Certificate of Achievement* onto card stock.

Description
The group participates in a sports activity together such as basketball or volleyball. Prior to beginning the game, the therapist reviews and explains the score sheet so the participants understand the behaviors that will be graded. The therapist selects one group member to be the scorekeeper (or alternates the scorekeeper by pulling one player from the game every five minutes.) The score keeper stays out of the game and observes the group playing the sport. The score keeper awards check marks for the behaviors listed on the score sheet. At the end of the game, the player with the most check marks is voted *Most Valuable Player* and applauded by the group and awarded a certificate. The group then discusses the qualities that make someone a *Most Valuable Player*.

Discussion
The *MVP* award is typically awarded to the player who is most athletic and/or most popular. However, in this activity, the *MVP* is awarded to the person who exhibits the best sportsmanship. Not only does this send an important message, but it also allows all children, regardless of their athletic abilities, to compete for a winning title. Moreover, in this activity, negative behavior is ignored and positive behavior is rewarded. Through this activity group members learn valuable social skills such as, friendliness, motivation, enthusiasm, and good sportsmanship.

MVP SCORE SHEET

PLAYER'S NAME	TRIES HARD	CHEERS ON OTHERS	FRIENDLY TO EVERYONE	FOLLOWS THE RULES

Certificate of Achievement

_____

(Child's Name)

This certificate is presented to you in honor of being voted

MOST VALUABLE PLAYER

Congratulations!

_____   _____

(Counselor's signature)   Date

FLIP A COIN

Theme: Social Skills
Recommended Age Range: Nine and Up
Treatment Modality: Small Group
Stage of Treatment: Middle

Goals
• Acquire awareness of socially acceptable behavior
• Provide opportunities for skill rehearsal

Materials
• Coin
• *Flip a Coin* skits (included)

Advance Preparation
Photocopy one *Flip a Coin* skits sheet for each client.

Description
Divide the group into two teams. Have one team begin by flipping a coin. If that team flips a Head that team picks a skit from the Heads column on the skit sheet and acts it out. The other team then acts out the same skit, but follows the guidelines from the Tails column. Each skit must have a beginning, middle, and end. The activity continues in this manner until all six skits have been enacted. Team members can take turns being actors and directors. Afterwards, the leader facilitates a discussion by asking the following:

What did you learn about inappropriate and appropriate behavior?
How do others react when you behave in a way that is socially unacceptable?
What did you learn today that you could try before the next session?

Discussion
This activity develops children's awareness of inappropriate and appropriate behaviors. It provides children with an opportunity to practice prosocial skills such as, being mature, assertive, polite, and respectful. Psychodrama is used to engage children in the activity and to encourage creativity among the group members.

Skits
FLIP A COIN

Heads

| Tails |

Heads

Make up a skit about being at a birthday party and acting **mature**.

Make up a skit about an argument with a friend in which you act **assertive** (you stand up for yourself in a non-violent way).

Make up a skit in which you are playing a board game with a friend and you **play by the rules.**

Make up a skit about peer pressure in which you **assert yourself** (stand up for yourself in a respectful, non-violent way).

Make up a skit about treating other kids with **respect**.

Make up a skit in which you are **polite** to your teacher.

Tails

Make up a skit about being at a birthday party and acting **silly**.

Make up a skit about an argument with a friend in which you act **aggressive**.

Make up a skit in which you are playing a board game with a friend and you **cheat** in order to win the game.

Make up a skit about peer pressure in which you **give in** to the pressure.

Make up a skit about **bullying** other kids.

Make up a skit in which you are **rude** to your teacher.

CHAPTER FIVE
SELF-ESTEEM

Most troubled children and youth suffer from a damaged sense of self. Some children have such profound self-esteem deficits that they have internalized the belief that they are bad and their future is hopeless. The goal of enhancing self-esteem for these troubled children is not an easy one, yet it is an essential component of any successful treatment program. In order to help children achieve this important treatment goal, various activities can be implemented from this chapter. These activities can be used as tools to help children focus on their strengths and abilities, promote feelings of self-worth, encourage a more optimistic attitude, and instill a message of hope for the future.

In order to be truly effective at strengthening a child's self-esteem, caregivers must be part of the process. Caregivers need to be taught and coached how to interact with their children in a positive way, as well as how to foster their children's unique talents. The activities in this chapter are, therefore, greatly enhanced by working in conjunction with caregivers.

HAPPY BIRTHDAY

Theme: Self-Esteem
Recommended Age Range: Four and Up
Treatment Modality: Small and Large Group, Family
Stage of Treatment: Middle

Goals
• Enhance feelings of uniqueness and self-worth
• Facilitate internalization of positive messages

Materials
• Birthday decorations (i.e., balloons, streamers, Happy Birthday banner)
• Party hats
• Blow horns
• Birthday cards
• Loot bags filled with party favors (see sample loot bag included)
• Adhesive labels for loot bag messages
• Party games (i.e., Piñata, Pin the Tail on the Donkey)
• Birthday cake with the following message: "Happy birthday to all you special children"

(**Note:** Decorations, hats, and cards can be homemade to cut costs)

Advance Preparation
Decorate the room with balloons, streamers, Happy Birthday sign, etc. Write a birthday card for each group member. Include a message about something that is special about the child in the card, for example, "I am so glad you were born because your smile brightens my day." Prepare the loot bags (see sample loot bag).

Description
The group leader states:

Today is a very special day. We are going to celebrate everyone's birthday. Even though it is not your actual birthday, we are going to celebrate your birth, because each of you is very special and worthy of being celebrated.

Party hats and blow horns are distributed to create a celebratory atmosphere. Birthday cards are read aloud, and birthday games are played (younger children can play Pin the Tail on the Donkey, teens can play dance music.) Lastly, the birthday cake is presented while the group leaders sing *Happy Birthday*. Loot bags are distributed to the children at the end of the session.

Variation for inclusion of caregivers: The children's caregivers can join the group. The group leader can ask each caregiver to write a birthday card ahead of time that they will read to their child during the birthday celebration.

Discussion

Helping children feel special, worthy, and valued is a tremendously powerful therapeutic intervention. Enhancing children's self-esteem is a major component of their healing process and it fosters their resilience. Children will enjoy the celebratory nature of this activity and hopefully integrate the messages of praise so they can establish a more positive sense of self.

This activity will be more powerful if caregivers participate. The therapist should meet with caregivers at least one week prior to the birthday session to assist them in writing the birthday cards to their children. Some caregivers will write loving and caring notes. Others may need guidance, and they can copy or modify a sample card prepared by the therapist.

SAMPLE LOOT BAG ITEMS AND MESSAGES

Star stickers: You are a shining star!

Silk flower: You have blossomed
into a wonderful person!

Gem stones: You are a precious gem!

Hockey or baseball cards: You're a sport!

Heart tattoos: You bring love and joy
to people around you!

Glitter glue: You sparkle!

TURNING OVER A NEW LEAF

Theme: Self-Esteem
Recommended Age Range: Nine and Up
Treatment Modality: Individual, Small Group
Stage of Treatment: Middle, End

Goals
• Encourage recognition of positive attributes
• Challenge and correct negative thinking
• Facilitate internalization of positive messages

Materials
• *One Negative Thoughts* questionnaire for each client (included)
• *Positive Thoughts* leaves (included)
• Green card stock or card board
• Scissors
• Treats (enough for all players)
• One *Changing Negative Thoughts to Positive Thoughts* sheet per client (included)

Advance Preparation
If the treats are a food item, then obtain permission from caregivers to offer food. Make a copy of the *Negative Thoughts* questionnaire for each client. Make a copy of the *Changing Negative Thoughts to Positive Thoughts* homework sheet for each client. Photocopy two copies of the two *Positive Thoughts* sheets onto green card stock and cut out the twenty-four leaves. Note that there are two of each so there is a matching pair for the game.

Description
Facilitate a discussion about negative and positive thoughts. Explain that negative thoughts are often untrue and exaggerated and when people think negative thoughts they feel bad, unlikable, nervous, and hopeless. An example of a negative thought is, "I'm no good." When people think positive thoughts, they feel confident, relaxed, and happy. Have the client give examples of negative and positive thoughts. Ask the client to do a self-evaluation by completing the *Negative Thoughts* questionnaire, then discuss the client's responses.

For the next part of the session, explain that the *Turning Over a New Leaf* game will help the client learn to challenge and replace negative thinking with positive thinking. Explain the game as follows:

This game is a memory game, similar to the memory games you may have played with picture cards or playing cards. However, instead of using picture cards or playing cards, this game uses positive thoughts to help us think positive. To play the game, players take turns turning over any two cardboard leaves to uncover the "positive thoughts". If the two leaves do not match, then they are turned back over. If the player makes a match, the player removes the two matched leaves and places them at her side. If the player matches positive thoughts she must indicate how that statement applies to her, then she gets a point for the match. For example, if the match is "There are things that I am good at" the player must tell about something that she is good at. If the player matches two blank leaves, she must give a compliment to each player. If she matches two leaves that say "Treat" she distributes a treat to each player. The player who finds the most pairs wins.

At the end of the game, the players can discuss how they can turn over a new leaf and think more positively.

Discussion

Troubled children often receive more negative feedback than positive feedback from parents, siblings, teachers, peers, and others. When children internalize this negative feedback they develop a negative self and worldview. They see themselves, others, and the world as bad. This negative thinking can lead to increased behavioral and emotional difficulties if left untreated. This activity assesses and challenges negative thinking and facilitates positive thinking.

Although most clients will enjoy the memory game, it can also create feelings of anxiety and inadequacy among children with a short attention span or poor memory skills. The therapist should be cognizant of participants' abilities and use this memory game with a group of clients who are at similar functioning levels. This game also involves reading so with younger clients the therapist should read the statements aloud as they are turned over during the game.

Questionnaire
NEGATIVE THOUGHTS

Below is a list of negative thoughts children may have about themselves, others, and the world. Read each thought and check off whether you never have that thought, have that thought a little bit, or have that thought a lot. There are no right or wrong answers; what's important is to show how you feel.

THOUGHT	I NEVER HAVE THIS THOUGHT	I HAVE THIS THOUGHT A BIT	I HAVE THIS THOUGHT A LOT
I'm no good			
I can't do well so there's no point in trying			
Nobody likes me			
I have never accomplished anything			
I can't trust anyone			
The world is a bad place			
People will think I'm a pest if I ask for help			
It's my fault my family is all messed up			
I will never be happy			
There's nothing I can do about my problems			

TURNING OVER A NEW LEAF
POSITIVE THOUGHTS

There are
things
that I am
good at

I can try my
hardest

There are
people who
like and care
about me

I can feel
proud of my
accomplishments

There are
people who
are kind and
trustworthy

I can think
about good
things that
happen

TURNING OVER A NEW LEAF
POSITIVE THOUGHTS

Everyone
needs help
with certain
things

Everyone in
my family plays
a role in making
it better

I can be
as happy
as I choose
to be

I can take
control of my
life and make
positive changes

TREAT!

106

Homework
CHANGING NEGATIVE THOUGHTS
TO POSITIVE THOUGHTS

What negative thoughts did I think today?

How did my negative thoughts make me feel?

What positive thoughts can I think instead?

How will these positive thoughts help me?

LABELS

Theme: Self-Esteem
Recommended Age Range: Nine and Up
Treatment Modality: Small Group, Family
Stage of Treatment: Middle

Goals
• Encourage recognition of positive attributes in self and others
• Encourage participants to look beyond physical appearance when establishing relationships
• Discuss the impact of positive and negative labels

Materials
• Adhesive labels (4"x 2")
• Markers

Description
Distribute the adhesive labels to the group members. Each participant should have the same number of labels as there are members in the group (i.e., if there are eight group members, then each participant should have eight labels). Have the participants "label" each other by writing complimentary attributes on the adhesive labels and sticking the labels on the shirt of the recipient of the compliment. Each group member should write one label for each participant. The complimentary labels must not be about physical attributes, so compliments regarding looks or clothing are not allowed. Examples that are discouraged are pretty, good dresser, nice hair, etc. Encourage labels such as, friendly, respectful, kind, etc.

Afterward, the group members read aloud their labels. The therapist facilitates a discussion by asking the following:

How does it feel to be positively labeled?
Why do you think compliments about appearance were discouraged?
What inner qualities do you value in others?

Discussion
Many children in counseling are used to being negatively labeled (i.e., bad, trouble maker, stupid, etc.) These labels perpetuate children's negative self-concept. This activity replaces negative labels with positive ones, thereby countering negative feelings and enhancing self-esteem. Moreover, since physical attributes are not allowed in the labeling activity, this game emphasizes and acknowledges personal strengths and inner beauty.

Note that this activity is most effective with an established group in which connections among members have developed.

LIGHT UP YOUR LIFE

Theme: Self-Esteem
Recommended Age Range: Twelve and Up
Treatment Modality: Individual, Small Group, Family
Stage of Treatment: Middle, End

Goals
• Identify negative and positive thought patterns
• Instill a positive attitude and a sense of hope

Materials
• Flashlight (one per client)
• Adhesive labels
• Wrapping paper

Advance Preparation
Write the following message on an adhesive label: "You can curse the darkness or you can turn on the light." Stick the message onto the flashlight and wrap it with the wrapping paper.

Description
Present the gift-wrapped flashlight to the client and discuss the meaning of the quote, "You can curse the darkness or you can turn on the light." Explain, "When things are going badly, you can dwell on the negatives or you can do something proactive to help yourself feel better. Each person has the power to choose darkness or light." The client can then identify ways that he can be proactive. For example, the client can make a list of positive memories, events, and achievements and then look at the list when having a bad day. The client takes the flashlight home and shines the light on the list to encourage an optimistic attitude.

Discussion
A few years ago, holocaust survivor, Gerda Klein, gave a lecture. She spoke of her horrendous experiences of loss and suffering at the hands of the Nazis. She also spoke about the end of the war, when she made the most important decision of her life: She chose to turn on the light, rather than to curse the darkness. Explaining stories like Gerda's to your clients may help them to feel inspired and understand that people can overcome adversity by having a positive attitude and by being proactive.

GIFT BAG

Theme: Self-Esteem
Recommended Age Range: Nine and Up
Treatment Modality: Individual, Group, Family
Stage of Treatment: Middle, End

Goals
• Understand the concept of self-talk and how it directs one's thoughts and behaviors
• Facilitate internalization of positive messages
• Encourage self-soothing behavior

Materials
• One gift bag per client
• Decorative supplies such as markers, glitter glue, colored felt, etc.
• Scissors
• One *Feel Good Message* sheet per client (included)

Advance Preparation
Copy one *Feel Good Message* sheet for each client.

Description
Explain the concept of self-talk by stating:

Most people carry on silent conversations with themselves; this is called self-talk. We tend to repeat the same messages to ourselves over and over, and soon, we come to believe these silent messages. For example, if I were to repeat to myself 'I can't do anything right,' I would soon believe this and this would make me feel badly about myself. On the other hand, if I were to repeat positive messages to myself such as, 'There are things that I do well,' this would help me feel better about myself.

Next, the client is provided with a gift bag and the list of *Feel Good Messages*. The therapist explains that the activity is to create a gift bag with positive messages. It will hold messages of hope and comfort that can be used when overwhelmed or in distress. The client then selects the desired messages, cuts them out, and places them in the gift bag. The client is encouraged to make up her own positive messages to add to the gift bag. The client can decorate the outside of the bag. The client takes the gift bag home and is encouraged to read through the messages in times of need.

Discussion

Most clients make negative, irrational, and self-defeating statements about themselves, which often leads to heightened feelings of worthlessness and anxiety. It is important to help clients learn how to use positive self-talk, so they can help themselves feel better when they are feeling anxious, discouraged, or inadequate. The gift bag can prompt clients to rehearse and memorize positive self-statements, so they have a repertoire to use when they are feeling upset or over-whelmed.

This activity can be used in the middle phase of treatment to address self-esteem issues, or it can be used as a termination activity to reinforce the client's positive attributes and progress in therapy.

FEEL GOOD MESSAGES

Fill your gift bag with *Feel Good Messages*. You can choose any from the ones below, or make up your own.

I can be good to myself

There are things that I do well

I am wiser and stronger now

My painful feelings are fading away a little each day

I can't change others but I can change myself

I can be grateful for all that I have

I can take pride in my accomplishments

I can follow my dreams

There are people who care about me

I am courageous

I can be as happy as I choose to be

PIZZA PARTY

Theme: Self-Esteem
Recommended Age Range: Seven and Up
Treatment Modality: Individual, Small Group
Stage of Treatment: End

Goals
• Recognize and honor progress made in therapy
• Facilitate expression of feelings regarding termination of therapy

Materials
• One *Pizza Party* worksheet for each client (included)
• *Pizza Party* puzzle (included)
• Scissors
• Small bag for cardboard pizza slices
• Dice (for group version)
• Party hats
• Transparent tape
• Pizza

Advance Preparation
Obtain permission from caregivers to offer pizza to the children.
Make a copy of the *Pizza Party* worksheet for each client. Photocopy the puzzle onto colored card stock and cut along the dotted lines to make six cardboard pizza slices. Place the six cardboard pizza slices in a small bag.

Description
The therapist introduces the activity by stating:

Today we are going to honor and celebrate the progress you made in this group by playing a party game. To do that, each of you will complete a worksheet, and then we are going to play a game called Pizza Party. At the end of the game, we get a special treat!

The therapist distributes party hats to the group members, creating a celebratory atmosphere. The therapist then distributes one *Pizza Party* worksheet to each group member for him to complete. Once the worksheets have been completed, group members sit in a circle with their completed worksheets in front of them. The bag filled with the six puzzle pieces is placed in the middle of the circle. The therapist explains the *Pizza Party* game as follows:

Players take turns rolling the die. They must answer the question on the worksheet that matches the number on the die. For example, when a player rolls three, that player shares his response for question number three on the worksheet ("Something I improved on"). All players then share their answer for question three. The player who rolled the dice then draws a cardboard pizza slice from the bag. Each cardboard pizza slice represents an item for a pizza. All six cardboard pizza slices must be earned in order to complete the pizza. The game is played until all six numbers of the die have been rolled and each of the six questions on the worksheet has been answered. If during the game, a player rolls a number that has already been used, the player rolls again until a new number comes up. When all the questions have been answered and the six cardboard pizza slices have been earned, the group puts the cardboard pizza puzzle together. The group is then awarded a special treat: pizza!

Party music can be played while the children eat their pizza to enhance the celebratory atmosphere in the group.

Variation for individual therapy: The worksheet is made into a puzzle by copying it onto colored card stock and cutting out the six pizza slices, each with a different question on it. The client writes an answer for each of the six questions, then puts the cardboard pizza puzzle together. As the client shares his responses to the questions, the therapist makes comments to affirm his achievements in therapy such as, "You have made wonderful progress!" The client is then provided with pizza as a special treat.

Discussion

This activity can be used in a final session as a creative way to affirm therapeutic gains. The activity also provides an opportunity to discuss the client's feelings about termination. The celebratory atmosphere that is created in the session facilitates a positive termination experience for clients.

WORKSHEET
PIZZA PARTY

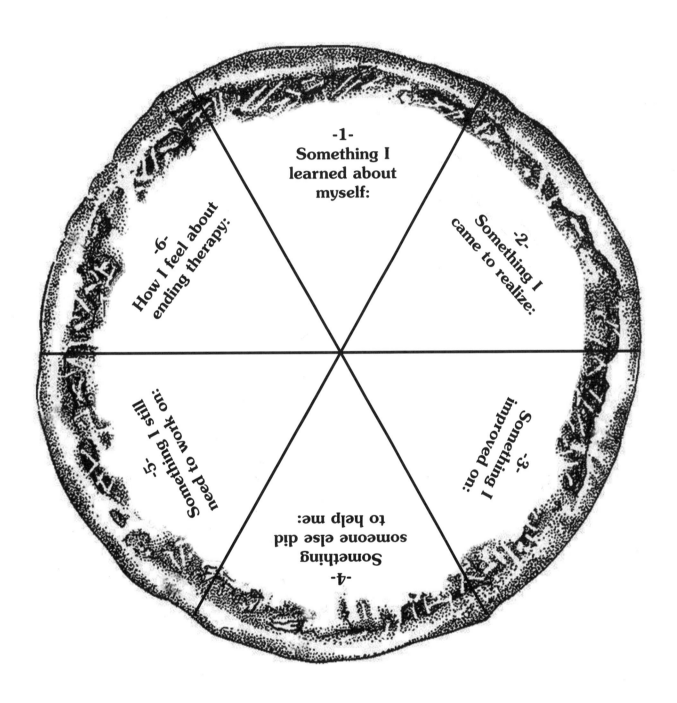

-1-
Something I learned about myself:

-2-
Something I came to realize:

-3-
Something I improved on:

-4-
Something someone else did to help me:

-5-
Something I still need to work on:

-6-
How I feel about ending therapy:

PIZZA PARTY PUZZLE

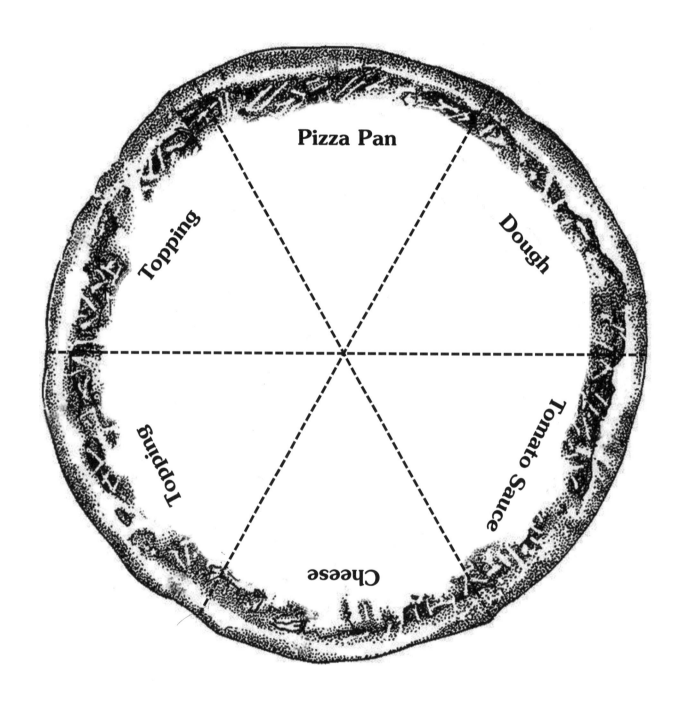

APPENDIX A

CHECK-IN AND CHECK-OUT ACTIVITIES

Check-In Activities

Having check-in rituals with clients at the beginning of sessions provides opportunities to connect with clients, build rapport, assess current functioning, facilitate self-expression, and bring structure to sessions. Below are some check-in ideas.

(Note: In order to be consistent, it is suggested that the same check-in activity be used each session.)

One To Ten
Clients rate their week on a scale of one to ten (one being terrible and ten being perfect).

Good Thing/Bad Thing
Clients report about one good thing that happened and one bad thing that happened during the week.

Feeling Face
Clients draw a feeling face to show how they feel (or have a sheet with a variety of feeling faces and clients can circle the faces and discuss their feelings).

Feelings Tic-Tac-Toe
Play a game of Feelings Tic-Tac-Toe which is published in the book, *Creative Interventions for Troubled Children & Youth* (Lowenstein, L. 1999. Toronto, ON: Champion Press.)

Check-Out Activities

It is important that clients leave each session with a sense of closure and a positive association with therapy. The check-out rituals below facilitate the closure process and enable clients to leave with positive feelings.

(Note: As with the check-in activities, it is suggested that the same check-out activity be used each session.)

Warm Fuzzy

Fill a clear jar with colored pom-poms (bags of assorted colors and sizes are available at craft stores). Label the jar Warm Fuzzies. At the end of each session, clients reach into the jar and select a pom-pom. Clients can decide whether they need a big warm fuzzy (large pom-pom) or small warm fuzzy (small pom-pom). The warm fuzzy is nurturing and serves as a good transitional object.

Joke Jar

Cut out strips of paper and write a joke on each paper strip (books with jokes appropriate for children can be found in the humor section of bookstores.) Fold the strips and place them in a jar labeled Joke Jar. At the end of each session, clients select a joke from the jar. Children can add their own jokes to the jar.

PEZ®

Have an assortment of PEZ® candy dispensers (available at candy stores) and at the end of each session, let clients choose a dispenser. Dispense a couple of PEZ® candies to the clients.

Affirmations Box

Cut out strips of paper and write an affirmation on each paper strip. Make up your own affirmations or copy from an affirmations book (i.e., *101 Affirmations for Teenagers* by Wardon and *Just Because I Am* by Payne). Fold the strips and place them in a box labeled Affirmations. At the end of each session, clients select an affirmation from the box. As an alternative, use a predesigned affirmations box, such as: *Magnify Your Magnificence* by Susan Howson (to order call 416-575-7836).

APPENDIX B

MANAGING CHALLENGING BEHAVIOR

Dealing with challenging client behaviors is one of the most difficult issues facing therapists. The child who is non-compliant, disruptive, aggressive, withdrawn, or unmotivated can provoke unpleasant feelings in therapists such as, frustration, anger, sadness, inadequacy, concern, and fear.

There are many reasons why children act out and there is always a message behind the behavior. Usually, the client's behavior is communicating an unmet need, for instance, a need to be engaged, empowered, nurtured, praised, heard, respected, etc. The mental health practitioner should try to decipher the message behind the client's behavior, so that the client's needs can be better addressed. In addition, there are several things the practitioner can do to prevent difficult behavior and intervene effectively when it arises.

Child Management Tips

- Pace sessions so clients do not act out in response to overly threatening material
- Captivate and sustain client motivation by making each session interesting
- Set realistic client goals and offer innovative rewards for achievement
- Treat all clients with acceptance and respect
- Model appropriate behavior
- Empower clients by involving them in formulating rules and consequences
- Be consistent and fair in enforcing rules and consequences, but not rigid
- Provide positive outlets for clients to channel their energy and tension
- De-escalate power struggles by staying calm
- Focus on and reward positive behavior
- Set up incentives to motivate and encourage positive behavior
- Explore the feelings behind the behavior
- Ensure each client succeeds at each session
- Recognize transference and countertransference issues
- Debrief with a skilled and approachable supervisor or colleague
- Self-care, self-care, self-care

Child Management Techniques

Rule Cards
Copy each rule onto a separate sheet of paper or cardboard (use a different color paper for each rule). Ensure that there are the same number of rule cards as there are group participants. Place the rule cards in a bag. At the beginning of each session, have each group member draw one card from the bag. Have each member identify and explain their rule card. For the duration of the session, if a group member breaks a rule, the person holding that card holds it up as a reminder of the group rules. If a group member breaks three rules during the session, that member is given a time out (or group members can establish an appropriate consequence).

For individual therapy, the rule cards can be taped onto the therapy room wall and reviewed during the first session. When a client breaks a rule during the session, the therapist can either point to the rule card as a reminder, or ask the client to identify which rule is being broken. Sample rule cards include:

Listen when someone is talking

Wait your turn

Talk nicely to each other

Be respectful of property

Keep one arm's length away from each other

Look people in the eye when they are talking

Have a positive attitude

Help each other

Help clean up

Tell the group leader if someone is hurting you

Group Jobs

Copy each Job from the list below onto a separate self-adhesive label. At the beginning of each session, assign one Job to each group member, or place the labels in a bag and have each group member pick a label from the bag. Have each member stick their label on their shirt and explain their designated Job. Suggested Jobs include:

Police Officer: Ensures all players are following the group rules.

Consequencer: If a group member breaks a group rule, the consequencer leads the group in a discussion about a fair consequence.

Cheerleader: Cheers the group on.

Praise Person: Praises group members for demonstrating positive behavior.

Summarizer: Summarizes what was learned during the session at the end of the activity.

Prize Distributor: Distributes a prize to each player.

Helper: Assists the group leader.

Cleaner: Cleans up at the end of the session.

Super Stars

Clients place a 4"x2" self-adhesive label on their shirts. During the session, the therapist places star stickers on the client's labels when they are behaving appropriately. At the end of each session, clients are awarded prizes based on the number of star stickers they accumulated.

1-10 stars = 1 prize
10-20 stars = 2 prizes
20+ stars = 3 prizes

Below is an excerpt from a group session illustrating this strategy:

(A group of four ten-year-old boys are playing a therapeutic board game.)
Rob: *It's my turn!*
Leo: *No it's not, it's my turn!*
Rob: *No stupid, it's my turn!*
Leo: (Shoves Rob) *You're such a loser!*
(Ian and Tim are playing the game without getting involved in Rob and Leo's conflict.)
Therapist: (Ignores Rob and Leo and places a star sticker on Ian and Tim's labels) *Ian and Tim, you're doing a good job following the group rules.*
(The game continues, and two minutes later, all group members are behaving appropriately.)
Therapist: *I like how everyone in the group is following the group rules right now.* (The therapist places a star sticker on each group member's label.)

In the above scenario, the practitioner ignores client misbehavior, and rewards positive behavior.

Secret Signal

Together with the client, develop discreet secret signals for use as cues and reminders of the rules. The cues can be visual or auditory. For example, when the therapist places a finger on her right ear, this signals the client to listen. When the therapist clears her throat, this signals the client to talk nicely to others. When the therapist holds out her arm, this reminds the client to keep a safe physical distance from others. Each signal should be reviewed to ensure that the client understands.

Stop Buddy

Divide the group members into Stop Buddy pairs. Explain the concept of a Stop Buddy as follows:

A Stop Buddy is someone who looks after his partner, and reminds him to Stop and Think before he acts out. For example, if someone teases you, you might feel like you want to hit that person. Your Stop Buddy will signal for you to walk away and cool off, so you don't act out and get into trouble.

Have each pair discuss other examples of when they can use their Stop Buddies. Next, have each pair create a discreet secret signal to cue their partner to Stop and Think. The pairs can then role play scenarios to practice being Stop Buddies.

Proud Bag

At the end of the session, clients tell about something that they feel proud of regarding their behavior. The positive statement can be written down and placed in a *Proud Bag*. For clients who need guidance, the therapist can provide fill-in-the-blank cards for them to complete. Sample cards include the following:

Today I learned...

Today I worked hard at...

I participated by...

I helped...

I listened when...

I showed respect when I...

I said a nice thing to...

I improved my...

BIBLIOGRAPHY

Child Development

Davies, D. (1999). *Child development: A practitioner's guide.* NY: Guilford.

Pine, F. (1985). *Developmental theory and clinical process.* New Haven: Yale University Press.

Child Management

Barkley, R., Edwards, G. and Robin, A. (1999). *Defiant teens: A clinician's manual for assessment and family intervention.* New York, NY: The Guilford Press.

Bowman, R., Carr, T., Cooper, K., Miles, R., and Toner, T. (1988). *Innovative strategies for unlocking difficult adolescents.* Chapin, South Carolina: YouthLight, Inc.

Schaefer, C. and Eisen, A. (1988). *Helping parents solve their children's behavior problems.* Northvale, NJ: Jason Aronson Inc.

Psychopathology and Trauma

Alderman, T. (1997). *The scarred soul: Understanding and ending self-inflicted violence.* Oakland, CA: New Harbinger Publications.

Eth, S. and Pynoos, R. (eds.) (1985). *Post traumatic stress disorder in children.* Washington, D.C: American Psychiatric Press.

Hindman, J. (1989). *Just before dawn.* Ontario, Oregon: AlexAndria Associates.

James, B. (1994). *Handbook for treatment of attachment-trauma problems in children.* NY: Free Press.

Janoff-Bulman, R. (1992). *Shattered assumptions: Towards a new psychology of trauma.* NY: Free Press.

Kendall, P. (2000). *Childhood disorders.* UK: Psychology Press.

Terr, L.C. (1990). *Too scared to cry: Psychic trauma in childhood.* New York: Harper and Row.

Walsh, F. (1996). "A concept of family resilience: Crisis and challenge", *Family Process.* 35(3), pp. 261-281.

Play Therapy

Bedard-Bidwell, B., and Sippel, M. (Eds.). (1997). *Hand in hand: A practical application of art & play therapy.* London, ON: Thames River Publishing.

Burns, M. (1993). *Time in: A handbook for child and youth care professionals.* Canada: Burns-Johnston Publishing.

Crenshaw, D, (2007). *Evocative strategies in child and adolescent psychotherapy.* New Jersey: Jason Aronson.

Crisci, G., Lay, M., and Lowenstein, L. (1997). *Paper dolls & paper airplanes: Therapeutic exercises for sexually traumatized children.* Indianapolis, IN: Kidsrights Press.

Di Leo, J. (1983). *Interpreting children's drawings.* New York: Brunner/Mazel.

Gil, E. (1991). *The healing power of play.* New York: Guilford Press.

Gil, E. (1994). *Play in family therapy.* NY: Guilford.

Gitlin-Weiner, K., Sandgrund, A, Schaefer, C. (Eds.) (2000). *Play diagnosis and assessment.* NY: John Wiley & Sons.

James, B. (1989). *Treating traumatized children.* Lexington, MA: Lexington Books.

James, O. (1997). *Play therapy: A comprehensive guide.* Northvale, New Jersey: Jason Aronson.

Kaduson, H.G., Cangelosi, D., and Schaefer, C.E. (Eds.). (1997). *The playing cure: Individualized play therapy for specific childhood problems.* Northvale, NJ: Jason Aronson Inc.

Kaduson, H., and Schaefer, C. (Eds). (2000). *Short-term play therapy for children.* NY: Guilford.

Kaduson, H. and Schaefer, C. (Eds.). (1997). *101 favorite play therapy techniques.* Northvale, NJ: Jason Aronson Inc. (*101 more favorite play therapy techniques* also available.)

Knell, S. (1993). *Cognitive-behavioral play therapy.* Northvale, NJ: Jason Aronson Inc.

Landgarten, H. (1987). *Family art psychotherapy: A clinical guide and casebook.* Levittown, PA: Brunner/Mazel.

Landreth, G. (1991). *Play therapy: The art of the relationship.* Muncie, IN: Accelerated Development Press.

Lowenstein, L. (1995). "The resolution scrapbook as an aid in the treatment of traumatized children." *Child Welfare.* 74 (4), pp.889-904.

Lowenstein, L. (1999). *Creative interventions for troubled children & youth.* Toronto, ON: Champion Press.

Lowenstein, L. (2006). *Creative interventions for bereaved children.* Toronto: Champion Press.

Lowenstein, L. (2006). *Creative interventions for children of divorce.* Toronto: Champion Press.

Lubimiv, G.P. (1994). *Wings for our children: Essentials of becoming a play therapist.* Burnstown, ON: General Store Publishing House.

McGuire and McGuire. (2001). *Linking parents to play therapy.* Brunner-Routledge.

Moustakas, Clark E. (1992). *Psychotherapy with children: The living relationship.* Greely, CO: Carron Publishers.

Oaklander, V. (1988). *Windows to our children: A gestalt therapy approach to children and adolescents.* Highland, New York: Gestalt Journal Press.

Ray, D., Bratton, S., Rhine, T., and Jones, L. (2001). "The effectiveness of play therapy: Responding to the critics." *International Journal of Play Therapy.* 10 (1), pp.85-108.

Rubin, J. (1984). *Child art therapy.* New York: Van Nostrand Reinhold Company.

Schaefer, C.E. and Reid, S.E. (Eds.) (1986). *Game play: Therapeutic use of childhood games.* New York: John Wiley and Sons.

Straus, M. (1999). *No talk therapy for children and adolescents.* NY: W.W. Norton.

Vargas, L.A. and Koss-Chiono, J.D. (Eds.). (1992). *Working with culture: Psychotherapeutic interventions with ethnic minority children and adolescents.* San Francisco: Jossey-Bass.

Group Psychotherapy

Corder, B.F. (1994). *Structured adolescent psychotherapy groups.* Sarasota, FL: Professional Resource Press.

Lennox, D. (1982). *Residential group therapy for children.* London: Tavistock Publications.

Northen, H. (1988). *Social work with groups.* New York: Columbia University Press.

Sweeney, D.S., and Homeyer, L.E. (1999). *The handbook of group play therapy: How to do it, how it works, whom it's best for.* San Francisco, CA: Jossey-Bass.

RESOURCES

Professional Associations

Canadian Association for Child and Play Therapy (CACPT) (Tel) 1-800-361-3951
2 Bloor Street West, Suite 100, Toronto, Ontario, M4W 3E2

Association for Play Therapy (APT) (Tel) 559-252-2278 (E-Mail) a4pt@sirius.com
2050 N. Winery Avenue, Suite 101, Fresno, California, 93703

Play Therapy International (PTI) (Tel) 613-634-3125
11E-900 Greenbank Road, Suite 527, Nepean (Ottawa), Ontario K2J 4P6

The American Art Therapy Association (Tel) 847-949-6064
1201 Allanson Road, Mundelein, IL 60060

Suppliers of Play Therapy Materials

Smilemakers (prizes and novelty items): 800-667-5000 (www.smilemakers.com)

Toys of the Trade: (prizes and small toys): 866-461-2929 (www.toysofthetrade.com)

Rose Play Therapy Toys (toys for therapy room): 800-713-2252 (play-therapytoys.com)

Ther-A-Play Products (toys for therapy room): 209-368-6787 or 800-308-6749

Enchanted Forest (puppets): 212-925-6677 or 800-456-4449 (www.sohotoys.com)

Centering Corporation (grief and loss): 402-553-1200 (centering.org)

ADD Warehouse (Attention Deficit Disorder): 800-233-9273 (www.addwarehouse.com)

PLAY THERAPY SUPERVISION AND TRAINING

- Do you provide counseling to children and adolescents?
- Are you interested in supervision and training in play therapy?
- Do you need supervision and training hours for certification or registration?

Supervision: Individual or group supervision is available for those residing in the Toronto area. Live "in session" supervision can also be arranged in our therapy center.

Long-distance telephone supervision: Supervision and/or consultation is provided by phone. Supervision is based on case discussion and/or review of video-tapes.

Clinical consultation: Consultation on hard-to-serve cases can be arranged in person or by telephone. Consultation on curriculum development for children's treatment groups is also available.

Training: In-service training throughout North America and abroad can be arranged on a variety of topics including: *Introduction to Play Therapy; Creative Interventions for Troubled Children; Innovative Assessment & Treatment Activities for Sexually Abused Children; Understanding & Helping Bereaved Children; Resolution Scrapbooks with Traumatized Children; Creative Activities to Enhance Family Interaction.*

BIOGRAPHY

Liana Lowenstein, M.S.W., RSW, CPT-S is a therapist and clinical consultant in Toronto, Canada. She is certified as a Child and Play Therapist and Play Therapist Supervisor from the Canadian Association for Child and Play Therapy as well as from Play Therapy International. Liana specializes in assessment and treatment services for children with a variety of emotional difficulties. In addition to her clinical work, she provides supervision, clinical consultation, and training to mental health professionals throughout North America and abroad. Liana is the author of numerous publications, including the books, *Paper Dolls & Paper Airplanes: Therapeutic Exercises for Sexually Traumatized Children, Creative Interventions for Troubled Children & Youth, and More Creative Interventions for Troubled Children & Youth.*

For further information, please contact Liana Lowenstein:
Email: liana@globalserve.net
Web: lianalowenstein.com
Tel: 416-575-7836

Innovative Child and Family Therapy Books

Creative Interventions for Troubled Children & Youth
By Liana Lowenstein
MORE Creative Interventions for Troubled Children & Youth
By Liana Lowenstein

These best-selling books are packed with creative assessment and treatment interventions to help clients identify feelings, manage anger, learn coping strategies, enhance social skills, and elevate self-esteem. They offer a wealth of practical tools for practitioners working with children in individual, group, and family counseling. Activities are geared to 4-16 year-old clients. **$25 US / $27 CDN**

Creative Interventions for Children of Divorce
By Liana Lowenstein

An innovative collection of therapeutic games, art techniques, and stories to help children of divorce express feelings, deal with loyalty binds, disengage from parental conflict, address anger and self-blame, and learn coping. Includes a theoretical overview and a reproducible handout to give parents. Also contains a ten-week curriculum that can be used in therapy or support groups. A much needed resource for counselors, therapists, and group facilitators. **$30 US / $32 CDN**

Creative Interventions for Bereaved Children
By Liana Lowenstein

A creative compilation of activities to help bereaved children express feelings of grief, diffuse traumatic reminders, address self-blame, commemorate the deceased, and learn coping strategies. Includes activities for children dealing with the suicide or murder of a loved one. Also contains a theoretical overview, tips for caregivers and teachers, and a ten-week curriculum for use in therapy or support groups. An invaluable resource for grief counselors, group facilitators, and school personnel. **$30 US / $32 CDN**

Paper Dolls & Paper Airplanes: Therapeutic Exercises for Sexually Traumatized Children
By Liana Lowenstein, Marilyn Lay, and Geri Crisci

This collection is brimming with more than 80 innovative activities for individual or group therapy with sexually abused children. Creative, engaging exercises help clients address issues such as feelings, disclosure, self-blame, offenders, triggers, sexuality, safety, and self-esteem. This best-selling treatment manual is an invaluable resource for practitioners working with sexually abused children, aged 4-16. **$40 US / $48 CDN**

Creative Family Therapy Techniques: Play, Art, and Expressive Activities to Engage Children in Family Sessions
Edited by Liana Lowenstein

Bringing together an array of highly creative contributors, this resource provides a unique collection of family therapy techniques. Authors illustrate how play, art, drama, and other expressive activities can effectively engage families and help them resolve complex problems. Practitioners from divergent theoretical orientations and work settings will find a plethora of innovative clinical interventions in this book. **$35 US / $39 CDN**

Assessment and Treatment Activities for Children, Adolescents, and Families:
Practitioners Share Their Most Effective Techniques
Vol 1, 2 and 3
Edited by Liana Lowenstein

In these three books, Liana Lowenstein has compiled an impressive collection of techniques from experienced practitioners. Activities address a range of issues, including feelings expression, social skills, self-esteem, and termination, and can be used in individual, group, or family sessions. A "must have" for practitioners seeking to add creative interventions to their repertoires **$25 US / $27 CDN**

Order Form

Name: _____ Agency: _____ Phone#: _____ Email: _____

Address: _____ City: _____ State/Prov: _____ Zip/PC: _____

How you heard about the books: ☐ Colleague (Colleague's name)_____ ☐ Ad (Cite AD#)_____ Other _____

☐ *Creative Interventions for Troubled Children & Youth :*
$ 25 US / $27 CDN QTY _____

☐ *More Creative Interventions for Troubled Children & Youth :*
$ 25 US / $27 CDN QTY _____

☐ *Creative Interventions for Bereaved Children:*
$ 30 US / $32 CDN QTY _____

☐ *Creative Interventions for Children of Divorce:*
$ 30 US / $32 CDN QTY _____

☐ *Paper Dolls and Paper Airplanes: Therapeutic Exercises for Sexually Traumatized Children :*
$ 40 US / $48 CDN QTY _____

☐ *Creative Family Therapy Techniques:*
$ 35 US / $39 CDN QTY _____

☐ *Assessment and Treatment Activities for Children, Adolescents and Families*
Volume 1 $ 25 US / $27 CDN QTY _____
Volume 2 $ 25 US / $27 CDN QTY _____
Volume 3 $ 25 US / $27 CDN QTY _____

Shipping charges: Orders under $50.00 = $7, orders over $50.00 = 15% of total. Canadians add 5% Tax on total.
All orders must be pre-paid. Cash or check payable to Liana Lowenstein. Total enclosed: _____
Mail completed form with payment to: Liana Lowenstein, PO Box 91012, 2901 Bayview Avenue, Toronto, ON M2K 1H0 Canada
For further information contact Liana Lowenstein: Tel: 416-575-7836 | Email: liana@globalserve.net | Web: lianalowenstein.com

ABOUT THE AUTHOR

Liana Lowenstein, MSW, RSW, CPT-S, is a Registered Social Worker and Certified Play Therapy Supervisor in Toronto, Canada. She maintains a private practice specializing in assessing and treating children with a variety of emotional difficulties. In addition to her clinical work, she lectures internationally on child trauma and play therapy. She is in the teaching faculty of the Canadian Association for Child & Play Therapy, and she provides clinical supervision and consultation to mental health practitioners. She is author of numerous publications including the highly-acclaimed books, Paper Dolls & Paper Airplanes: Therapeutic Exercises for Sexually Traumatized Children (with Crisci & Lay), More Creative Interventions for Troubled Children & Youth, Creative Interventions for Children of Divorce, and Creative Interventions for Bereaved Children. For further information about the author, upcoming workshops, or to order books, visit: www.lianalowenstein.com